Walking Around Loch Ness,
The Black Isle and Easter Ross

Some 'old' walks
and some 'new'.
Hope you will enjoy them!

Love. June.   Feb '14

Clan Walk Guides

Walking Around Loch Ness, The Black Isle and Easter Ross

Walking Scotland Series
Volume 17

Mary Welsh
and
Christine Isherwood

First published by Clan Books, 2010

ISBN 978 1873597 33 0

The authors wish to express their gratitude to Jennifer Outhwaite
and Dr Catherine Isherwood for their help in preparing this volume

**Clan Books
Clandon House
The Cross, Doune
Perthshire
FK16 6BE**

Printed and bound in Great Britain by
Bell & Bain Ltd., Glasgow

Publisher's Note

Our new volume replicates many of the characteristics of the previous one, which explored the lands from the source of the Spey to the Buchan coast. This one extends far to the west, east and north of its epicentre, Loch Ness. The contrast between the terrain lying to the west of the Great Glen and that to the east and north of it is dramatic. The latter areas are quite well populated with farming and other rural activities interspersed with forestry and natural woodland, on each side of the regional capital, Inverness. Between Loch Ness and the west coast is a vast, beautiful wilderness of mountain, loch and river, teeming with wildlife but notably short of human habitation.

This area is largely the preserve of extensive sporting estates. Nowadays, visitors wishing to walk the hills and glens are generally welcome, but there is an obligation during the limited stalking season (mainly between mid-August and mid-October) for walkers to respect the way of life of these communities, using the various telephone helplines before starting out, to ensure that they do not cause problems or endanger themselves where deer stalking is scheduled to take place.

The Authors' Golden Rules
for Good, Safe Walking

- Wear suitable clothes and take adequate waterproofs.
- Walk in strong footwear; walking boots are advisable.
- Carry the relevant map and a compass and know how to use them.
- Carry a whistle; remember six long blasts repeated at one minute intervals is the distress signal.
- Do not walk alone, and tell someone where you are going.
- If mist descends, return.
- Keep all dogs under strict control. Observe all "No Dogs" notices – they are there for very good reasons.

Contents

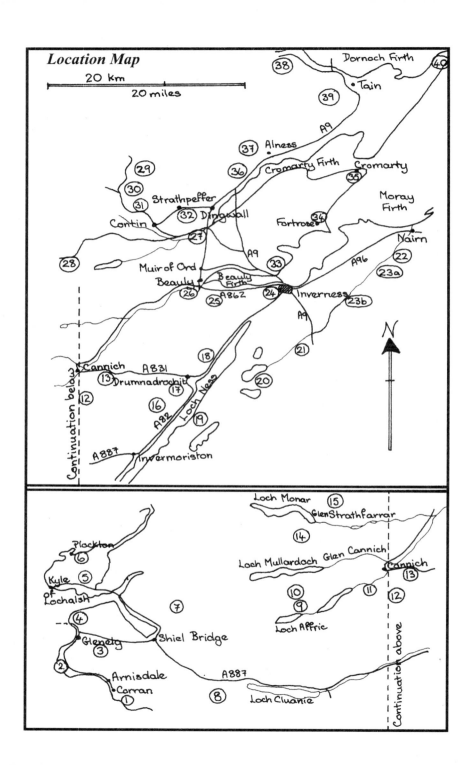

Location Map

20 km

20 miles

1

Corran and Loch Hourn

Park in the car park on the right, almost at the end of the public road, grid ref 849093. To reach this leave the A87 at Shiel Bridge and take the minor road south over the Mam Ratagan Pass to Glenelg. Continue along this road to drive through Arnisdale on Loch Hourn and on to the end.

Loch Hourn forms the northern boundary of Knoydart. It is a beautiful fiord-like loch surrounded by high mountains. Access by road is difficult; there is a minor road along by Loch Quoich to Kinloch Hourn at the head, and this road which crosses the high pass of the Mam Ratagan. Remote, delightful Arnisdale and Corran lie on the loch's northern shore, looking south to the mountains of the Knoydart peninsula. Corran is famous for Sheena's Tea.

1 Carry on to the end of the road and cross the bridge over the River Arnisdale. Look for grey wagtails in the burn and herons where it flows out into the loch. Bear right and walk past the cottages of Corran; the

Luinne Bheinn, Loch Hourn

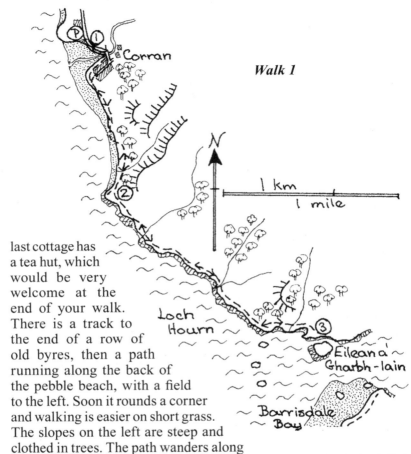

Walk 1

Corran

Loch Hourn

Eilean a' Gharbh-lain

Barrisdale Bay

last cottage has a tea hut, which would be very welcome at the end of your walk. There is a track to the end of a row of old byres, then a path running along the back of the pebble beach, with a field to the left. Soon it rounds a corner and walking is easier on short grass. The slopes on the left are steep and clothed in trees. The path wanders along the top of the beach then up a path into the trees and winds delightfully along a shelf before descending to a gate in a deer fence. Then it goes out onto the beach again and back onto the grass. Oystercatchers pipe at the water's edge, and you may see otters. The views up Loch Hourn to Sgurr a'Choire-beithe and Luinne Bheinn, and across the loch to Ladhar Bheinn (Larven) are spectacular. The intimidating ridge ending in a seamed vertical wall of rock is Stob a'Chearcaill on Ladhar Bheinn.

2 The path bends inland (a faint one goes right here) and climbs a little to go above a small headland. There are fewer trees now and the path can be quite boggy in places after rain. It goes down to another bay and on round the edge. Carry on along the pleasing way, fording several

small burns on stones. Eventually
the path runs through a narrow
defile in the cliff, then out
to a shallow bay where it
comes to an end, but it
is possible to continue a
little farther until you are opposite a
tidal island, Eilean a'Gharbh-lain. Look
across the loch to Barrisdale Bay with its
wide sands and magnificent surrounding
mountains. Loch Hourn suddenly becomes
much narrower beyond this point, and there is no longer a
way along the north shore.

Oystercatchers

3 When you are ready to leave this delectable spot retrace your
   steps to Corran and your car. Enjoy the splendid views down the
   loch to Beinn Sgritheall towering over Arnisdale and out across the
   sea to the Cuillin.

Heron

Practicals

*Type of walk: This is a lovely there-and-back walk on the same
route, with superb views along the shore of one of Scotland's more
remote sea-lochs. The path is clear although somewhat wet in
places.*

Complete distance: 4 miles/6.5km
Time: 2–3 hours
Maps: OS Explorer 413/Landranger 33

2

Sandaig (Gavin Maxwell's Camusfearna)

There is room for several cars on the edge of the road where the forest track goes down, grid ref 783151. To reach this, leave the A87 at Shiel Bridge and cross the Mam Ratagan Pass to Glenelg. Continue past the village and on for about 4 miles to a forest track on the right just before a lochan.

Sandaig is better known to most people as Camusfearna, the remote house and bay where Gavin Maxwell lived for ten years with his tame otters, first Mijbil and then Edal, and told their story in the book 'Ring of Bright Water'.

Sandaig

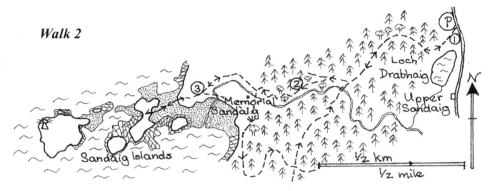

Walk 2

1 Walk on down the track round the edge of the reedy lochan. You may see herons here, and look for teal and mallard in the overgrown fringes. The track passes an area of beech trees then goes on into spruce. Ignore a track to the right, but at the next one, where you can hear the burn just a short distance ahead, turn right. Take a well-used but unsigned path on the left 22yds/20m along this track. It runs above the gorge in which the burn flows, and can be muddy in places after rain. At first the path descends gently and the burn below gets further away as it plunges over unseen waterfalls. On reaching a viewpoint enjoy the superb vista out over Sandaig Bay and the islands. Look for the small lighthouse on the outermost island to Skye, where you can see Isle Ornsay Lighthouse, which also belonged once to Gavin Maxwell.

2 After this, the path becomes much steeper, and you need to hold on to trees beside it. At the bottom, cross a fence by a stile and walk on beside the burn. There is a deep ford with stones and a double rope across to help you if you wish to cross here. Otherwise follow the path up onto the wave-cut platform and then round above the burn to reach the cluster of tidal islets. If you are here at low tide it is a wonderful area to explore with craggy outcrops of rock and sandy bays littered with shells. Seals haul out on the outer rocks and if you are lucky you may see an otter. Oystercatchers pipe wildly from the rocks and green-shanks feed in the edge of the waves at the right time of year.

Greenshank

11

Common Seal

3 If the river is not too high you may be able to cross, probably by paddling, and explore the far side. The house in which Gavin Maxwell lived is no longer there but there is a memorial, and you can walk up by the burn to see the waterfall and pool where his tame otters used to swim. Then you will either have to ford the burn again to return by your outward path, or if the forest operations have finished, go through a gate beside some ruined walls onto a good path leading up into the trees. It winds right and joins a forest road at a viewpoint where again you can look down on the bay and islands. Go on up to a cross of tracks where you turn left. Cross the bridge over the burn and rejoin your outward track to return to the road.

Wood Sorrell

Practicals

Type of walk: Mostly good tracks although the path down to the bay is quite steep and muddy in places. Forest operations at the time of writing restricted access to the return path but should soon be finished.

Complete distance: 2½ miles/4km

Time: 2–3 hours

Maps: OS Explorer 413/Landranger 33

3

Glen Beag and the Brochs

Park in the large layby by Dun Telve Broch, grid ref 829173. There are several other places along the glen if this is full. To access this, leave the A87 at Shiel Bridge and cross the Mam Ratagan Pass to Glenelg. A mile beyond Glenelg take the very minor road on the left up Glen Beag, signed to the Brochs.

A **broch** is a fortified, circular tower, dating back to around 1000BC. Located in the glen south of Glenelg are two of the finest found on the Scottish mainland. They have an outer and inner shell, with floors of galleries formed of large slabs within. They may have had a conical roof. The two are set in idyllic surroundings and are very interesting.

Dun Telve (broch)

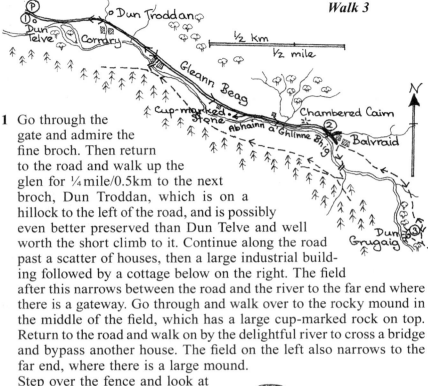

Grey Wagtail

1 Go through the
gate and admire the
fine broch. Then return
to the road and walk up the
glen for ¼ mile/0.5km to the next
broch, Dun Troddan, which is on a
hillock to the left of the road, and is possibly
even better preserved than Dun Telve and well
worth the short climb to it. Continue along the road
past a scatter of houses, then a large industrial building followed by a cottage below on the right. The field
after this narrows between the road and the river to the far end where
there is a gateway. Go through and walk over to the rocky mound in
the middle of the field, which has a large cup-marked rock on top.
Return to the road and walk on by the delightful river to cross a bridge
and bypass another house. The field on the left also narrows to the
far end, where there is a large mound.

Step over the fence and look at
the mound; it is the remains of a
chambered cairn and one of the
chambers can still be seen although
it has collapsed. The views up the
glen as you walk are very pleasant.
Look for grey wagtails and dippers in
the burn, and buzzards soaring above.

2 Carry on along the road to its end
at Balvraid and take the right
fork here, as directed by a small
sign to Balvraid Broch. Go past
a farm building, then keep left at
another fork and wind across open pasture to cross a burn at a
paved ford. Climb the hill beyond and look over to the right to see
the ruins of the third broch, Dun Grugaig, less well preserved than the
other two. Where the road levels out take a small path, which crosses

14

the high ground to the broch. It is built on a steep rocky knoll with a sheer drop down to the river on the far side and is a most spectacular site. There is a fine view back down the glen to the Skye hills.

3 Return down the track towards Balvraid farm, but at the junction passed earlier turn left towards the river. There is a bridge, which at the time of writing is distinctly ricketty, although still obviously in use by the farmer. If you don't like the look of it or it has fallen down or become very unsafe you will have to walk back along the road to your car, or paddle which is possible unless the river is in spate. Otherwise cross with care and turn left at the end to wind round right on an old grassy track running up the field to a gate into the forest. Go through and turn right along a delightful mossy track, which runs between alders along the bottom edge of the forest, with lovely views out over the glen. Eventually this joins another track; turn right and cross another bridge in a rather better state of repair, and walk left along the road to your car.

Oak and Alder

Practicals

Type of walk: Very pleasant on a very minor road and tracks. Lots of archaeological interest.

Complete distance: 4 miles/6.5km

Time: 2–3 hours

Map: OS Explorer 413/Landranger 33

4

Glenelg to Ardintoul

Park in the car park above the ferry terminal to Kylerhea, grid ref 795213. To access this, leave the A87 at Shiel Bridge and cross the Mam Ratagan. Before you reach Glenelg village take the road on the right signed to the Skye Ferry to Kylerhea.

Cross on the summer **Kylerhea ferry** to Kylerhea Otter Haven. The crossing is exciting and from the Haven there are spectacular views across the narrows to where you have walked and of the Kintail mountains. It is an ideal otter habitat with resident wild otters. Otter cubs spend the first 18 months with their mother, learning how and where to catch prey, and how to behave as otters. For details contact 01320 366322.

Old Boat Winch, Ardintoul

1 Walk out of the car park along the path signed to Ardintoul and Totaig (SRWS). Go through two gates close together; then the pleasant way winds in and out through heather and scattered birch. Beyond a deer gate the track enters conifers and climbs slightly. Take the left branch, marked with an arrow of stones at a Y-junction, and go downhill to pass directly below a huge pylon taking the power cables across the narrow strait to Skye. At the far side the track becomes a path, running along a shelf

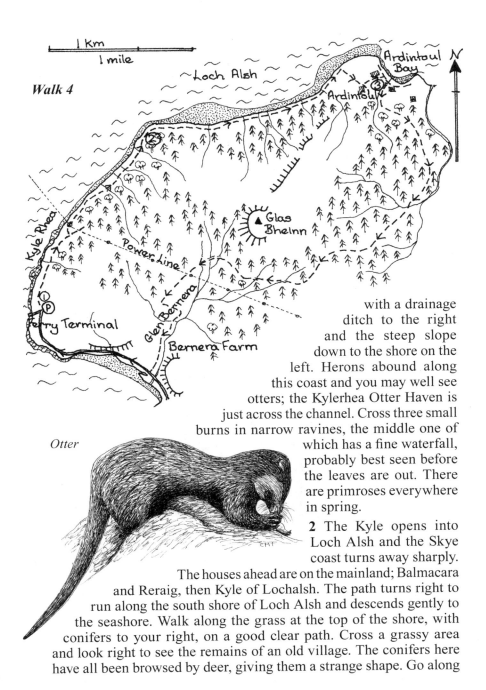

Walk 4

1 Km
1 mile

~Loch Alsh

Ardintoul Bay

Ardintoul

Glas Bheinn

Power Line

Kyle Rhea

Glen Bernera

Ferry Terminal

Bernera Farm

N

Otter

with a drainage ditch to the right and the steep slope down to the shore on the left. Herons abound along this coast and you may well see otters; the Kylerhea Otter Haven is just across the channel. Cross three small burns in narrow ravines, the middle one of which has a fine waterfall, probably best seen before the leaves are out. There are primroses everywhere in spring.

2 The Kyle opens into Loch Alsh and the Skye coast turns away sharply. The houses ahead are on the mainland; Balmacara and Reraig, then Kyle of Lochalsh. The path turns right to run along the south shore of Loch Alsh and descends gently to the seashore. Walk along the grass at the top of the shore, with conifers to your right, on a good clear path. Cross a grassy area and look right to see the remains of an old village. The conifers here have all been browsed by deer, giving them a strange shape. Go along

17

between the shore and the conifers again to another open area divided into fields. Keep to the outside of the wall past two fields then take a grassy track running inland away from the sea, through a gate and on to join a more well-used track. Turn left and walk down past a large white house to regain the shore. This is Ardintoul.

3 Turn right onto another track, which runs above the shore towards a white cottage. Bear right past the cottage and ignore the next left turn. The track winds slightly uphill with a burn and a fine overgrown beech hedge to the right. Cross a cattle grid and begin to climb. The track is metalled wherever the gradient is steep, but for the rest it is just reinforced. The first part is the steepest but it keeps on climbing for a long way. Eventually it swings right and then left; a small path from the highest point, the Bealach Luachrach, will take you to the top of Glas Bheinn should you want to add more to the walk. Otherwise continue down the long slope winding round the hillside between conifers and into Glen Bernera. The track turns left and crosses the glen, then winds right beside the burn where you might see grey and pied wagtails. Go on down to join the road. Turn right and follow the narrow road above a splendid sandy bay, which you may like to visit, and then go on round below cliffs to the Kylerhea Ferry and the car park.

Primroses

Practicals

Type of walk: Good paths and tracks and a short stretch on a public road, which may be busy at ferry times. Lovely views.

Complete distance: 8 miles/13km

Time: 4–5 hours

Maps: OS Explorer 413/Landranger 33

5

Kirkton and Balmacara Square

Park in the large space by the church at Kirkton, except when there is a service, or by the hall, grid ref 829272. Access is along the A87 towards Kyle of Lochalsh and about 1 mile west of the junction with the A890.

The **badger** is a nocturnal animal though it is sometime seen abroad during the day. Generally it emerges after sunset and returns home at dawn. For its size it is immensely strong and very active when awake, but it has the gift of sleeping soundly in a completely relaxed way. It is omnivorous, living on lizards, mice, voles and young rabbits. It also eats beetles, earthworms, slugs and will dig out nests of bumble bees. It will take acorns, beech mast, grass and clover and dig for succulent roots.

Badger

The **Great Spotted Woodpecker** 'song' is believed to be the loud mechanical 'call', a vibrating rattle, produced by rapidly repeated blows of its strong bill upon a trunk or branch. The sound travels a long way depending on the wind direction and the condition of the wood. A hollow bough produces a louder note than living wood. The neat round nesting hole is bored into soft or rotten wood, horizontally for a short way and then down a shaft of about six inches. In a chamber at the foot of the shaft, lined with wood chippings, five or six white eggs are laid towards the middle of May.

Great spotted woodpecker

1 Cross the road and take the signed path to Balmacara almost opposite. Go through a kissing gate and follow the path uphill with a burn to the right. It swings left and goes down into a hidden valley. Look for badger footprints in the mud, and you may see a great spotted woodpecker. Go through a gate, cross the valley floor then walk round the next gate or climb the stile beside it. After 50 yards further on turn right on a waymarked path leading uphill into a larch plantation. The path climbs steadily, then comes to the edge of a burn in a gorge and zigzags steeply up the side of the ravine. The trees here are oak and birch, and the views are splendid, both into the gorge and out east across Loch Alsh to the hills.

In Balmacara Square

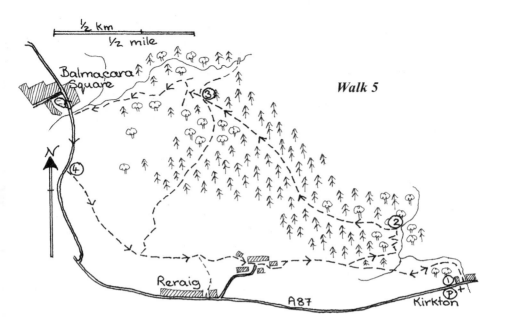

Walk 5

2 Eventually the path turns away from the gorge, runs across the hillside and up a last slope then begins to descend gently beside an old wall. Another brief climb brings you onto a delightful terrace path running along the hillside through open oak and birch woodland and gradually going downhill. From time to time there are conifers enclosing the path, where you may see goldcrests and siskins. Through the trees there are glimpses across Loch Alsh to Skye.

At the next junction you can turn left for a shorter walk. This takes you through mature beech wood at first, then past a small concrete dam and into more ordinary forestry plantation. Follow the well-made path until it comes out through a gate into open heath land with gorse, then to the remains of a military installation. The view from here is spectacular. Turn left onto a metalled road and wind downhill until it joins a reinforced track. Turn left.

3 If you want to do the longer walk keep straight ahead at the above-mentioned junction. Follow the waymarks down to cross a forest track, then take the left path at a Y-junction. Carry on downhill crossing the burn twice on footbridges. Turn right onto another forest track, then left at a corner to rejoin the path and finally walk down a fenced way beside the burn to the road at Balmacara Square. Turn right and have a look at the Square, which is a delightful village complete with pond. Then walk back down the road to take a left turn, signed to Reraig, about 300 yards beyond the path you came on.

4 This track climbs steadily between gorse until it reaches the track on the left, which was the short cut. Go straight ahead, gradually descending. Ignore a path on the right which goes down to Reraig, and continue through scattered trees with lovely views out to the south and west. Cross a bridge over a small burn and go through a kissing gate onto a metalled road. Carry on in front of several cottages, passing a signpost where you follow the sign to Kirkton. At the end of the tarmac ignore a road going right and follow the sign for a small footpath, also on the right, before a house entry. The path goes round the outside of the garden and rejoins what was obviously the continuation of the track. This goes along through open ground with scattered trees, through a gate and below the forest to rejoin your outward route at the point where the path went up into the woodland. Continue to the main road and cross to your car.

Goldcrest

Practicals

Type of walk: Most enjoyable. On good paths and tracks. Some steep climbing near the start.

Complete distance: Short walk 3miles/5km:
Longer walk 4½ miles/7km
Time: 2–3 hours
Maps: OS Explorer 413/Landranger 33

6

Plockton and Duncraig

Park in Plockton on the right side of the shore road, grid ref 803333. Access is by minor roads, over the hill from Balmacara Square, or from Kyle of Lochalsh or from the A890 at Achmore.

Plockton lies towards the seaward end of Loch Carron. Cottages hug the shore of this idyllic village. Palm trees line the main street, framed by a landscape of pines and heather and from here you have superb views of the Wester Ross mountains.

Originally named **Am Ploc**, it was a crofting hamlet until the 1700s. Then the landowners found they could make more money by letting the land to sheep farmers. The crofters who had lived there for generations were cleared and most had to emigrate. The herring boom came and the population of the hamlet increased to over 500, many living two families to a cottage. Then the herring boom ended. This

Plockton

23

was followed by the potato famine and Plockton became known as the village of the poor.

With the arrival of the **railway** in the 1890s Plockton's fortunes improved. In the mid 1990s the BBC filmed three series of **Hamish Macbeth** and tourists flocked to see the village. The highlight of the year is the Annual Plockton Regatta.

About the middle of the 19th century the Free Church of Scotland split from the main body of the Church of Scotland, and the worshippers in Plockton found themselves without any building in which to hold their services. They converted a **natural amphitheatre** in the rocks into an outdoor church until they had raised enough money and were able to build a new church down in the village – now converted to dwellings.

1 Walk back up the main road out of the village, past the Primary School. Look on your right for the open-air church, and go up the steps and through the arch to see it. Return to the road and continue along the pavement until houses appear ahead, then take a signed path on the left. Follow it down steps and across duckboards round the head of a long narrow sea inlet. The delightful way runs along between the shore and the railway line, with the steep slopes to the right covered with feather moss, ferns, and primroses in spring. The path climbs up opposite Plockton to cross a rocky knoll, with the railway down below in a cutting, the path then descending again. Go through a gate followed by a tunnel under the railway and carry on along the other side. The path then turns away from the railway and begins to climb.

2 At a junction take the signed left turn to

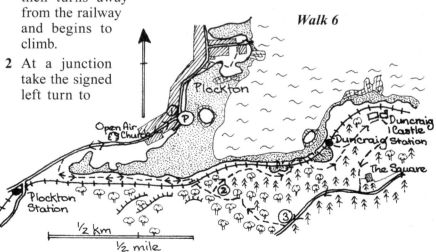

Heron

Duncraig Castle. Go through a small gate and on downhill. This path runs through several tunnels of rhododendrons and can be quite muddy and wet. Cross an open area of larch trees, festooned with lichens, with a ruin at the far side and an enclosed sea inlet on the left. At the end take a path, left, down an awkward step. Go through another tunnel under the railway to follow a path above the shore. The views are beautiful with beaches and rocky islets crowned with pine trees. Herons frequent the shore. At the next junction keep right to a gate and crossing over the railway and turn left at the far side. The path is difficult for a short way, very muddy and overgrown with rhododendrons; keep right and soon it improves. Go round another, much larger, enclosed sea inlet then uphill at the far side to join a metalled road. Turn left and take the left branch at a Y-junction to look at Duncraig station with its attractive octagonal station building. Then return along the road to walk in front of the partly derelict Duncraig Castle by cutting across the edge of the grass on a faint track or keeping to the tarmac, before going up the approach road, past the Square to the public road and turn right.

3   Soon the road runs between big old beech and lime trees. Look for a signed path to Plockton on the right and follow it downhill through large mature oaks and lovely birchwood. The way is well made and relatively dry. Go past the turn to Duncraig Castle, taken on the way out, and follow the path under the railway and back above the shore to Plockton, enjoying the views over the village to the Applecross hills.

Practicals

Type of walk: Distinct paths all the way but in the rhododendrons before Duncraig Castle it can be very muddy. There are usually ways round.

Distance: 3 miles/5km

Time: 2–3 hours

Maps: OS Explorer 428/Landranger 24

7

The Falls of Glomach

Park in the small forestry car park at Dorusduain, grid ref 978223. To access leave the A87 at the north side of the causeway 2 miles/3.2km beyond Shiel Bridge, to take a minor road to Morvich. Go past the cemetery, then after ½ mile/1km take a private road on the left. Do not worry about the private signs. Watch out for speed bumps. Continue along the road into the forest.

The Allt a' Ghlomaich, **the Burn of the Chasm**, rises on high ground north of Beinn Fhada. The mountain river issues from the lowest of three lochs and eventually plunges over the Fall of Glomach into Glen Elchaig below Loch na Leitreach. It is Scotland's premier waterfall because of the height of its unbroken fall. It is generally held to be the second highest at 350ft/106m. The highest is Eas a'Chual Aluinn in Assynt, but Glomach has a much higher volume of water and is much the more impressive of the two.

The Falls were presented to the National Trust, in 1941, by Hon G B Portman of Inverinate and Mrs Douglas of Killilan. After her long tramp to the falls, **Brenda Macrow** in her book **Kintail Scrapbook** says "I turned away, feeling that if I stayed any longer I should be dazed by the noise and drawn down into the black chasm below." She goes on to describe them as "Sombre, barren, with a wild, distinctive beauty, they are well worth the effort expended in reaching them." But the authors of this book stress that the utmost care is required to enjoy their magnificence.

1 Walk round the gate and up the track to the left of the entry to the car park, following a sign for Falls of Glomach. Ignore a left turn; the track soon levels and goes on through serried conifers with glimpses of A' Ghlas Bheinn and Beinn Fhada through openings in the trees. There are both pine marten and fox droppings on the path and on stones. Go through a gate in a deer fence. Ignore a track on the right,

Falls of Glomach

e M Isherwood

then one on the left. Cross a bridge over the Allt an Leoid Ghaineamhaich to climb gently on the other side of the burn. Descend to cross a bridge over a tributary burn, where the forest track ends. There are attractive waterfalls in both burns. Climb steeply up a pitched path on the far bank, which zigzags to help reduce the gradient. The slope then eases and the path winds along the side of a long glen with the amazingly seamed side of

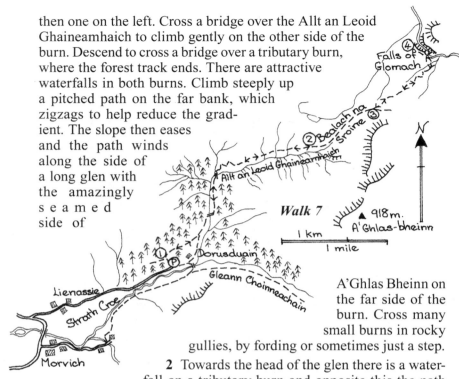

A'Ghlas Bheinn on the far side of the burn. Cross many small burns in rocky gullies, by fording or sometimes just a step.

2 Towards the head of the glen there is a waterfall on a tributary burn and opposite this the path ascends a spur, taking you up out of the main glen to a notch at the top, the Bealach na Sroine. Cross the burn at a well-made crossing point and follow the path out of the notch and up onto a wide plateau, where there are splendid views across to the Affric hills and north to the hills beyond Glen Elchaig. It feels very far away from civilisation. The path is marked by many cairns, the sign of an old coffin route. It winds along the side of the hill to avoid the boggy ground. Listen for golden plovers' plaintive call, and look out for deer.

3 Head for a prominent knoll, beyond which the ground falls steeply away into Gleann Gaorsaic. The top of the falls, where the river suddenly disappears, is obvious and you can hear the roaring. The path descends a spur in tight zigzags, and is pitched in the steeper places. Very soon you are down at valley level. Check to make sure you will remember which of the several spurs is the one you came down, then bear left across a wide boggy area, keeping back from the river to avoid peat hags. A notice tells you that the falls are extremely dangerous and warns you to take great care. Follow the path, now stony again, along

above the dizzying ravine. There is a small, exposed but good path zigzagging down the side from which you can get a better view of the fall, but you cannot see all of it. It is immense, divided part way down by an outcropping rock, and then vanishing into the narrow chasm below. Do take care; people have been fatally injured here, and it is no place for anyone without a head for heights. But if you can manage to look, it is absolutely spectacular and well worth the effort involved in getting there, especially a few days after heavy rain.

Golden plover

4   When you have seen your fill make your way back across the bog to the spur you came down. Go back up and retrace your steps across the plateau and down the long valley, enjoying the view from the top across to Beinn Sgritheall and Beinn a'Chapuill.

Practicals

Type of walk: Long and into lonely country. The paths are good except for a short boggy stretch just before the falls, but because of the remoteness and the height, over 1650ft/500m on the plateau, you should go well prepared with waterproofs, good boots, map and compass. Do take care near the waterfall where the ground is extremely precipitous. The route traverses the Inverinate estate. During the stalking season it is advisable to check possible access problems with the estate office (01599 511303/250).

Complete distance: 7½ miles/12km

Time: 4 hours

Maps: OS Explorer 414/Landranger 33

8

On the South Cluanie Ridge

Park in the large car park across the road from the Cluanie Inn, grid ref 077118. If using a second car leave it in the large layby at grid ref 043116. Access this by the A87 from Invermoriston to Glen Shiel.

The **South Cluanie** (or South Kintail or South Glen Shiel) Ridge is a superb ridge of seven Munros and two tops, which encloses Glen Shiel on its south side. The side facing Glen Shiel is sculpted into huge dramatic corries, but the other hidden side above Glen Quoich is grassy and more rounded. The ridge only drops below 2600ft/800m in one place (not included in this walk) and many fit walkers do the whole magnificent traverse in one day.

1 Cross the road and walk east along the small path beside it for 660ft/200m to the junction with the old road to Tomdoun. Turn right along this road to cross the Cluanie River and then swing left above Loch Cluanie. After 980ft/300m from the bend the road crosses a burn; shortly before the bridge look for a small but quite distinct stalkers'

On the South Cluanie Ridge (Aonach Air Chrith from Druim Shionnach)

30

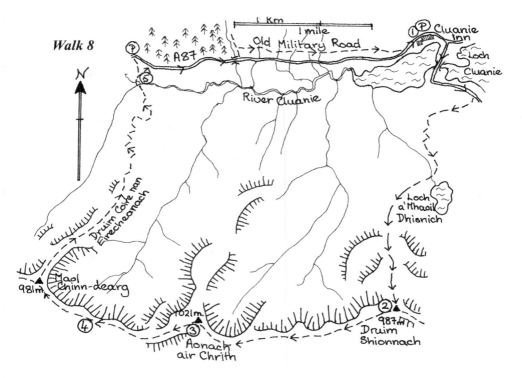

Walk 8

N

1 Km
1 mile

Old Military Road →

(P) Cluanie Inn

A87

Loch Cluanie

River Cluanie

Loch a'Mhaoil Dhisnich

Druim Coire nan Eirecheanach

Maol Chinn-dearg
981m

1021m

Aonach air Chrith

Druim Shionnach
987m

path ascending a spur of the hill on the right, and follow it as it winds upwards. It makes for excellent walking. Pause at intervals to admire the unfolding view of the Kintail mountains. The path crosses a burn (the outflow from a lochan, Loch a'Mhaoil Dhisnich, and the last water you are likely to find until you are nearly down to the road again) on large flat stones and a few metres farther on it disappears. Carry on up the ridge, making use of the gravelly terraces for easier walking. You can see the lochan in its hollow below you as you ascend. Ahead the way seems blocked by a band of crags but a small path winds round to the left; it involves a little easy scrambling but soon you reach less steep ground and continue up the broad ridge to the summit cairn of Druim Shionnach. This is the second Munro on the South Cluanie Ridge; the first one, Creag a'Mhaim, is a mile away to the left. If you want to include this in your walk, turn left and descend a short steep rocky section, probably easiest if you keep to the ridge rather than the vertiginous bypass path, and from there go along the easy broad path. This will add an hour to your walk, and you have to return over the top of Druim Shionnach, but the drop is only 336ft/120m.

2   To continue along the ridge, walk west from Druim
    Shionnach along a gentle grassy path. There are
    splendid crags falling into the corrie on your
    right and steep slopes to the left. In spring
    these hold snow patches and on a hot
    day you may see red deer sitting on
    the snow. Look out for ring ouzels
    and listen for their blackbird-like
    song or alarm chatter. Go
    over a small interme-
    diate top and then
    by-pass the next
    one on a clear
    path leading down to a low
    col. Climb again to the summit o f
    the next Munro, Aonach air Chrith, the highest point on the ridge,
    which has a splendid rocky spur heading north.

Ring ouzel

3   Leave the summit by its western ridge which is also steep and rocky;
    some of the steps down are quite big, requiring sitting down (for
    some) to descend, but it is not difficult. However it is quite narrow and
    exposed. Look back when you reach the col to admire the slabs on the
    side of Aonach air Chrith. The views from here are very fine, with the
    Loch Quoich hills across the valley and Knoydart to the west, then all
    the mountains south to Ben Nevis to the south-east, and Kintail to the
    north.

4   The ascent to your last Munro, Maol Chinn-dearg, is very straight-
    forward. Turn right from its summit cairn to follow the excellent path
    down its grassy north ridge. There are a couple of steepish sections
    near the top, then a broad level plateau. At the end of this join a stalk-
    ers' path and descend in wide easy-angled zigzags all the way down
    to Glen Shiel; it must be one of the most pleasant descents in Scotland.
    Cross a burn on stones at the bottom (the stones are very large; it is
    easy normally but could be difficult if the burn is in spate), then another
    burn where you have to jump. Walk up the path towards the road.
    Where the path divides take the right branch if going back to Cluanie
    Inn; the left branch leads up to a layby where you could be met or leave
    a second car.

5   To return to Cluanie Inn, turn right and walk with care along the edge
    of the road until you reach the end of a plantation on the far side. Cross
    over, go across the bridge over the burn and turn left up a path on its
    far side. Carry on up here to a ruined sheepfold, and turn right along

an indistinct track which is an old military road. This is actually quite hard to see on the ground at first but becomes much clearer as you get nearer to the inn, and is much pleasanter than trying to walk all the way back on the busy main road. It joins the road 100yards/91m short of the inn. Continue to the car park.

Mountain Azalea

Practicals

Type of walk: This is a splendid climb; save it for a good day and go well prepared with waterproofs, good boots, map and compass. There are a couple of rocky sections and one place where the ridge is quite narrow, so if you have no head for heights you may not like it, but it is not difficult. The views are superb and the path down is a joy. At the outset you will pass notices advising you to keep to the paths and ridges during the stalking season, but if in doubt ring the estate office (01599 511282).

Complete distance: 10 miles/16km
Time: 7–8 hours depending on fitness
Maps: OS Explorer 414/Landranger 33

9

Loch Affric

Park at the River Affric car park, grid reference 201234. This lies at the end of the minor public road to Glen Affric leaving the A 831 at Cannich. Turn right just past Fasnakyle Power Station.

Glen Affric was part of the **Clan Chisholme** lands. Before the Clearances life was very hard for the families here trying to survive by subsistence farming on very poor soil. Consequently from around the 1780s landowners, receiving a poor financial return, forced the families out of the glen to make room for a more remunerative occupant – sheep. The glen became a vast sheep run.

Sheep caused damage to the pine forest. Deer, introduced to the Glen for shooting parties, also added to this. Timber was also extracted from the glen for shipbuilding and to fuel iron smelters. But in spite of all this there is still a large area of ancient Caledonian forest. In 1951 the Forestry Commission purchased a large part of Glen Affric and 2001 it received National Nature Reserve status.

A charity, **Trees for Life**, have a re-planting programme in the area, to restore the Caledonian Pine Forest. Volunteers come periodically throughout the year to help with conservation projects.

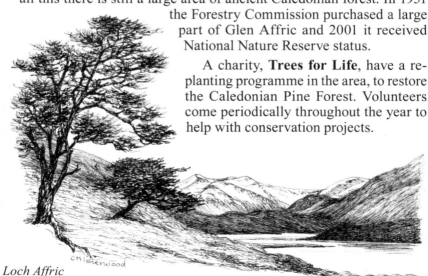

Loch Affric

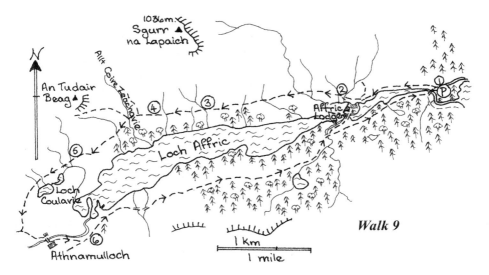

1 Leave the car park by the entry and turn sharp left; take the right hand fork to head along the north side of the glen. Follow this vehicle track for about a mile through open birch woodland until it bends left to go to Affric Lodge, with another track zigzagging right up the hill. Here take a narrow signed footpath, which follows the outside of a deer fence. Cross a small burn on a single rather bouncy plank, which can be slippery if wet but usually the stream is shallow enough to be crossed on foot if you prefer not to risk the plank.

2 The footpath rejoins a track that comes through the deer fence. Look down to the loch here for a view of Affric Lodge. You may see a green-shank by the water's edge. Cross an open area, to a deer-fenced enclosure, part of the native forest regeneration scheme for Glen Affric, to prevent access by deer in order to give the tree saplings a chance to grow. Go through the pedestrian gate and walk on through the scattered granny pines and now frequent pine and birch saplings. The puddles may be full of frog spawn or tadpoles in the spring.

3 The path reaches a place where it has become quite washed out. Make your way across this to the burn which usually flows across the path. Under normal conditions it is easy to pick a way across on stones. Continue along the footpath as it climbs a little; there is a lovely view across the upper part of Loch Affric, with mature Caledonian pine forest on its shores, to the fine mountains at its head. Keep a lookout for red deer above the fenced enclosure to the right. You may also see Scottish crossbills flying between the scattered pine trees.

4 Just beyond the crest of the climb, you reach the end of the deer-fenced enclosure with another pedestrian gate. Go through and follow the path as it descends gently, keeping to the left fork at the junction. Shortly, cross a large burn on a solid bridge. Then the path descends for a while and gives clear views of the head of the loch. Listen for cuckoos calling in spring. Look right to see a spectacular waterfall, Sputan Bàn, leaping down the steep hillside above you. There is no bridge where this river, the Allt Coulavie, crosses the track, but under normal conditions it is easy to cross dryshod on stones, either at the ford or a little higher upstream. However, it is subject to rapidly changing levels after high rainfall or through melting snow and can be impassable when in spate. Please take care. If the water level is too high, the safest option is to return by your outward route.

Crossbill

5 Once across the Allt Coulavie, follow the track through an open area of hummocky moraine in Glen Affric. Look out for goldeneye on Loch Coulavie down to your left. You may also be lucky enough to see a golden eagle circling up above you. Beyond the loch the track climbs gently before winding down to join another track. (Turning right here would lead on to Alltbeithe youth hostel and across to the West Coast.) This walk turns sharp left, which takes you down towards the River Affric and Athnamulloch bothy. Cross the river on the large wooden bridge and take the small footpath which leaves along the river bank to the left. This brings you to a small burn with a narrow wooden plank bridge, which you take to join the main vehicle track from Athnamulloch. Continue along the track as it follows the river, then climbs up the hillside a little to meet another track.

6 Bear left at the junction and continue round the hill below birch woodland. As you come over the crest of the hill pause to enjoy the spectacular view down Loch Affric. Go on into another deer-fenced enclosure with new saplings and granny pines. Then the track leads downhill, past a small boggy lochan and towards the Allt Garbh. Cross the river on a bridge and go through the pedestrian gate in the deer fence. The enclosed area to the left of the track here is part of the private policies of Affric Lodge, just across the loch. Walk on past a cottage and uphill to go through another gate; head on into more mature pine forest. This is another good area to look for crossbills flying across the track or feeding in the tree tops. You may also see crested tits. After a while the track heads downhill again; follow the left branch down to the river. Go through the gate and cross the bridge. At the far side leave the track to take a small path to the right; this winds steeply up through the young trees to bring you into the main car park.

Red Deer stag

Practicals

Type of walk: Fine long walk, relatively level, and all on tracks or good footpaths. There may be difficulty crossing the Allt Coulavie. If in spate, go back the way you came. This route is unlikely to be affected by stalking activities, but if in doubt ring the estate office (01465 415350).

Complete distance: 10 miles/16km.

Time: 5–6 hours

Maps: OS Explorer 414 and 415/Landranger 25

10

Tom a' Choinich

Park in the car park where the public road crosses the Abhainn Gleann nam Fiadh, near the west end of Loch Beinn a' Mheadhoin, grid ref 217242. Access this along the minor road from Cannich in Strathglass to Loch Affric.

Tom a' Choinich (the mossy hill) is 3669ft/1112m high and is a fine hill with a curving ridge enclosing a high corrie on the eastern side. To the west a ridge continues to Carn Eige and Mam Sodhail and eventually to the hills above the Falls of Glomach. The pass between Tom a'Choinich and its eastern neighbour Toll Creagach, the Bealach Toll Easa, was once a well-used way between Glen Affric and Glen Cannich, but the creation of Loch Mullardoch cut off the Cannich end of the path.

1 Cross the road and walk up the glen, following a good track with a pine forest to your right. On a sunny day butterflies are abundant along this stretch and you may see both small pearl-bordered and high brown fritillaries. Go through a deer gate into young forest. There are views

Tom a' Choinich

c. M Isherwood

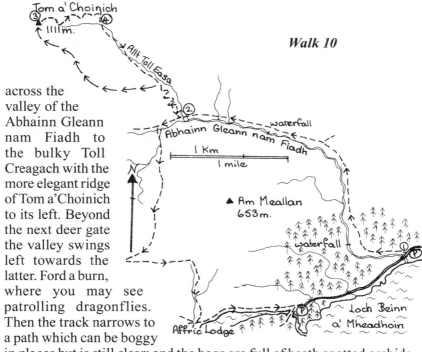

across the valley of the Abhainn Gleann nam Fiadh to the bulky Toll Creagach with the more elegant ridge of Tom a'Choinich to its left. Beyond the next deer gate the valley swings left towards the latter. Ford a burn, where you may see patrolling dragonflies. Then the track narrows to a path which can be boggy in places but is still clear; and the bogs are full of heath spotted orchids in summer.

2 Cross another burn, (the Allt Toll Easa, on stones and turn right beside it to ascend a path on the far bank. This is an old stalkers' path and makes wide zigzags to ease the gradient. As you approach the lip of the corrie take a small but distinct path going off on the left. It winds round crags and up onto a rocky ridge which leads gradually and pleasantly up to the main spine of the mountain. The going becomes easy on short grass and gravel, and soon you reach the summit. There are splendid views of Carn Eighe and Mam Sodhail to the west, and north to the Mullardoch hills. Look along the skyline for golden eagles.

Golden eagle

3 When you are ready to leave take a small path descending a short ridge, which runs

39

east from the summit towards Toll Creagach, the nearest hill, a big rounded lump. The path soon leaves the rocky top of the ridge and winds down its southerly side in wide zigzags. Look for alpine flowers; moss campion, alpine lady's mantle, starry saxifrage, bearberry and dwarf cornel. Then the path regains the ridge crest and descends to the col between Tom a' Choinich and Toll Creagach. You can see the old path going on north winding round the flank of Tom a'Choinich on its way down to Loch Mullardoch; nowadays it goes no further because the loch is artificial.

Dwarf Cornel

4 Turn right to go down the corrie from the col, following a good path, which winds in and out by the burn over pleasant turf with occasional wet patches. At the lip of the corrie rejoin the path you came up and continue down to the river, the Abhainn Gleann nam Fiadh. Turn right and cross it if the river is not too high; if it is in spate you also may not be able to cross it a little higher up and need to walk up the glen to an obvious crossing point. Ford it here on convenient stones and climb the path up the far side onto the plateau between Sgurr na Lapaich and Am Meallan. There are splendid views up Glen Affric as you come over the top. The path makes a wide sweep round and then descends gently down the escarpment, finally zigzagging down to the path along the north side of Loch Affric. Turn left and follow this path until it joins the road, and then back to your car.

Practicals

Type of walk: A most enjoyable climb on good paths, with occasional boggy places. Superb views. If there has been a lot of rain it may not be possible to ford the Abhainn Gleann nam Fiadh in which case return by your route of ascent. In the stalking season, to check possible access problems beyond the forest boundary, call the estate office (01320 366322).

Complete Distance: 10 miles/16km

Time: 6–7 hours

Maps: OS Explorer 415/Landranger 25

Coire Lochan and Dog Falls

Park at Dog Falls car park, grid reference 287284. To reach this drive up the minor road to Glen Affric from the A831 at Cannich, turning right at Fasnakyle Power Station. The car park is on the left of the road.

Beautiful, secluded **Coire Lochan** lies in a sheltered hollow in woodland. It is an important breeding site for many species of dragonfly.

Dog Falls has been described as spellbinding, also as fascinating, the latter because it can never be viewed in its entirety. From the footbridge it roars away at the far end of the gorge. From the viewpoint the first part of its great fall can be seen. But it is well worth a visit and the walk to see it and the loch is a delight.

Dog Falls

1 Leave the car park and cross the forestry bridge over the River Affric. Go through a pedestrian gate in the deer fence and walk on, climbing gently through beautiful Caledonian pine forest with some majestic granny pines, the veterans of the pine forest, which is home to an amazing array of species. Look in summer for common wintergreen, a pine forest speciality. The track sweeps round a corner to the left and levels out; shortly afterwards there is a small path leading off left to a viewpoint over the glen.

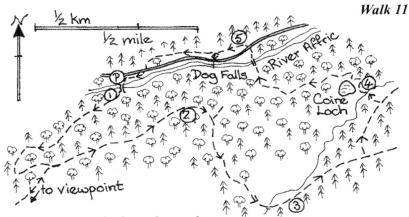

Carry on up and where the track divides, take the left-hand branch.

2 Further on the track bends right and begins to descend gradually. Ignore a waymarked path leaving down to the left and continue along the main track as it heads into a sheltered dip. This area contains a much greater mix of trees, mostly deciduous, including oak and hazel. Soon the area to the right becomes more open, a result of clear-felling to remove planted conifers and encourage the regeneration of native trees. As you walk, look for dragonflies flying in the sunshine, sometimes coming to rest on the warm track surface; these can include some rarities such as white-faced darter and azure hawker which have a stronghold in the area.

Common Wintergreen

3 Soon the track heads uphill again. Take the path leading off left, signed 'Coire Lochan'. This narrower, more overgrown way leads you through the open pine forest until suddenly you can see the Coire Lochan very close on the left. The loch is in a small marshy hollow, surrounded by *Sphagnum* bog, which is now partly colonised by small pine trees. Look for the dabchicks that nest on the loch, and listen for their distinctive trilling calls. Watch also for dragonflies and damselflies, for which Coire Lochan is renowned, in particular the downy emerald dragonfly, which has huge green eyes.

4 As you head on round the loch, look for crested tits in the mature pine trees before the path starts to climb the hill to an open rocky ridge from where there is a lovely view across the loch and on over the head of Strathglass.

Dabchick

Perhaps this is the place for your picnic. Then continue along the foot-path, pausing to admire the majestic veteran oak tree off to your right. This area is much more open, with a fine mix of trees. Go on along the path heading down to the River Affric. Walk on to the wooden bridge over the river and look up the gorge towards Dog Falls, and then go on up to the road which you should cross with care.

5 From here follow a path, left, through more pines. At a signed path turn left down to the Dog Falls viewpoint. Cross the road again and look over the wooden fence to the top of Dog Falls at the head of the Affric gorge. Then walk back up to the main path. Turn left to continue along the footpath above the road for a while, then wind down to cross the road again before heading along beside the river. Look out here for dippers and grey wagtails, which can often be seen bobbing on the rocks in the river. The path brings you back to the car park.

Practicals

Type of walk: Lovely walk through forestry with much wildlife interest, especially on a warm sunny day when the dragonflies can be spectacular. All on good paths and tracks, and well waymarked.

Complete distance: 4 miles/6.5km
Time: 2–3 hours
Maps: OS Explorer 415/Landranger 25

12

Plodda Falls

Park in the forestry car park for Plodda Falls, grid reference 280238. To access this drive through the conservation village of Tomich, south of Cannich in Strathglass where you turn off the A 831. Carry on for 3 miles/5km, taking the left fork at a junction just beyond the village and then again about a mile further on, after passing a steading and a cottage. Here the left fork is reinforced but not metalled and it continues like this for the rest of the way. The large white house beyond the fine lily pond is Hilton Lodge. Soon after passing its road end you reach the car park on the right for Plodda Falls. There are signs for the falls all the way.

The glory of the **Plodda Falls** is amazing. The burn descends steeply, with an awesome roar, through soaring trees including great firs planted in the 1880s by Lord Gladstone. The falls are on a tributary, the burn Eas Socach, of the River Deabhag, the latter lying in a deep gorge far below and the burn having to make a sensational descent (Plodda Falls) to join it.

Plodda Falls

1 Walk out of the far end of the car park down a forestry track to a group of waymarks and posts. Ignore the path going left and carry on down the track, following green markers. At a junction with another track, walk on straight ahead (the right branch) down the older way, through splendid tall Douglas firs. Turn left down the next waymarked path and descend stone steps to a T-junction, where you turn right. This path runs along above a dry gully filled with luxuriant ferns, including large banks of beech fern. Lower down a burn develops in the gully, and the path carries on above it, down through an open grassy area with scattered birch to join a track near a house at the bottom.

Walk 12

Abhainn Deabhag

Tomich

waterfall
Plodda Falls

¼ km
¼ mile

2 Turn left and walk along the track through more magnificent Douglas firs, until you reach a turning place with a path going left. Carry on ahead to look at the old ford over the burn, which here flows relatively peacefully. There are huge trees above the cliff on the far bank. Then return to the path, now on your right, and climb the stepped way with the burn to your right. There is a platform on the right from which you can see the top of the falls. At a junction turn right down steps, with a firm fence on your right, to reach a viewpoint below the falls, and very close to them. If there has been much rain they are magnificent but be prepared for a shower bath.

3 Return to the main path and continue climbing, taking the right branch at a junction and then again to follow the fence. At the top of the falls the Forestry Commission has now built a superb viewing platform to replace the unsafe bridge; walk out along this for a vertiginous view of the water roaring away over the cliff beneath your feet. It is a most amazing experience.

4 Return to the path and carry on up. Cross a track, admiring a smaller but still spectacular (after rain) fall on the burn, then take the left path to climb steeply through bilberry and heather to rejoin the track on which you set out. Turn right to the car park.

Crested tit

Practicals

Type of walk: Short and interesting, especially good after rain. All on good paths and tracks.

Complete distance: 1½ miles/2.5km
Time: ½–1 hour
Maps: OS Explorer 415 /Landranger 25

13

Corrimony

Park in Corrimony Cairn car park, grid ref 384302. This lies 24 miles/38km south-west of Inverness. It is well signposted off the A831 8 miles/13km miles west of Drumnadrochit.

The **Corrimony Neolithic chambered cairn** was constructed about 4000 years ago and is known as a passage grave. The original structure would have had a high central chamber completely roofed and entered by a low passage. Also it would have been surrounded by a ring of kerbstones. In the 1950s excavations revealed the remains of one person, possibly that of a woman. When it was no longer needed, so many centuries ago, it is believed that a low wall was built round it and then the whole enclosed in a stone circle. Today it stands in a grassy area shaded by trees and is a delightful corner from which to start this walk.

The **nature reserve** is open at all times and the route is mainly waymarked. Loch Comhnard, in the summer months, attracts common sandpipers, greenshanks, curlews and ospreys. In winter look for goldeneye and whooper swans. Also watch out for black grouse among the heather and young birch.

Chambered Cairn, Corrimony

1 Walk on for a hundred yards from the parking area to visit the Cairn. Then return to the road and carry on. Follow it as it winds right and then left to come close to the placid River Enrick. Ignore a ford and a fine stone bridge and continue on to cross the river on a wide flat bridge. Go through a gate and stroll along an avenue of splendid mature trees.

2 At the end of the avenue turn left and descend to cross a tiny tributary (sometimes just mud) on stones and then ascend the pastures on a good track. Bear right to go through double gates into the nature reserve and on up for a short way to reach the top corner of the pastureland, just before the start of a pine forest on the right. Here turn left into the forestry to stroll a grassy ride. This continues pleasingly before winding right, high above the River Enrick. At the bend, look down, with care, to see the river far below. Carry on the lovely high-level way until you reach a distinct path, left, through the trees, level at first and then zigzagging steeply down through the pines, the latter providing good hand-holds, to reach an old path along a shelf well above the Enrick. Turn right and walk a short way towards the sound of tumbling water and then to view the magnificent Corrimony falls.

3 Return up to the high-level path, then right to reach the main track and turn left to climb up through the pine forest. (If you are feeling in an exploratory mood, walk a short way left along the high-level path, then take, right, an indistinct path and sometimes no path at all, through the pines, over rough ground underfoot, to reach the main track and turn left.) Go on gently climbing, pausing occasionally to look back over the superb landscape. Then leave the pine forest behind and move out into a high open area, where a few elderly birches stand up above many thriving young trees and heather.

48

4 Finally you reach the high-level heather moorland, where a few fenced areas have been planted. At the brow of the track you have your first glimpse of Loch Comhnard almost encircled by dark heather-clad mountains. Then descend steadily through the moorland to sit beside the loch for some bird watching or your picnic lunch.

5 Retrace your outward route, remaining on the track until you reach the double gates out of the reserve. Do not pass through but step right to join a delightful, grassy path, with a fence to the left. This takes you at first high above the river and then comes to a bench seat from where you might wish to sit and enjoy the wonderful tranquility of the lovely glen. Then continue gently descending to where the path comes beside the river, now wide and flowing gently over its pebbly bed. Follow it as it winds left, and brings you to a gate onto the track once more. Turn right, cross the flat wooden bridge and stroll on to the parking area.

Black Grouse

Practicals

Type of walk: Good tracks and paths. Take care on descending to waterfall. The track over the moorland can be bleak so choose a good day.

Complete distance: 6 miles/9.5km
Time: 3–4 miles
Maps: OS Explorers 415 and 416/Landranger 26

14

Toll an Lochain, An Riabhachan

Park on the area of hard standing just below Misgeach power station at the end of the surfaced road up Glen Strathfarrar, grid ref 183381. To access this, drive along the private road through Glen Strathfarrar from Struy on the A831 in Strathglass. Cross the Monar Dam (the turn for this is abrupt just after passing an outcrop of rock on the left), and continue to the power station.

For access to the glen ask at the gatekeeper's cottage by the locked gate at Inchmore, just up the glen from Struy, for permission to enter. This is available from 9 am to 5pm; last exit depends on day length, 6pm in April and October, up to 8pm in June, July and August. The glen is closed all day Tuesday, and Wednesday morning until 1.30 pm. In winter, November to the end of March, the glen is closed and entry

Sgurr na Lapaich and
Toll an Lochain

is by prior arrangement with the gatekeeper, tel 01463 761260, or by contacting the Mountaineering Council for Scotland on 01738 638227 in good time to make a booking. During the stalking season July 1 to October 20, ring the hillphone on 01463 761360.

An Riabhachan is a high, remote Munro on the ridge between Loch Mullardoch and Glen Strathfarrar. It has a fine narrow summit ridge but is otherwise grassy apart from the splendid wild rocky corrie, Toll an Lochain, the aim of this walk, where two lochans nestle in an exciting and dramatic situation below the cliffs.

The Monar Dam, which considerably increased the size of remote Loch Monar, is part of the hydro-electricity scheme in the Beauly catchment area. The water from this and from Loch Beannacharan lower down the glen goes by tunnel to two underground power stations at Deanie and Culligran.

1   From the parking area, return along the road to the hairpin bend and bear left along a good track. Continue up the glen until it approaches the river, Uisge Misgeach, at a weir and a slightly ricketty bridge, both crossing a tributary burn, the Allt Coire na Feithe. Go over the bridge, with care, and on up the narrower path ahead towards a flight of waterfalls, which are spectacular when the river is in spate. After ½ mile/1km beyond the bridge take a path, left, which returns you to the riverside. The river is now called the Allt Doire nan Gillean. Then carry on along a narrow footpath on the bank to the right. At the confluence of the

Walk 14

two burns cross the Allt Doire nan Gillean on stones and continue on the clearer stalkers' path as it heads uphill beside the tributary, the Allt an Eas Bhàin Mhòir.

51

2 The path follows the burn until the way becomes steeper, where it strikes off to the right at an easier angle across the slope. It then zig-zags up the steep hillside. As you gain height turn round to look at the spectacular view of Maoile Lunndaidh and Sgurr a' Chaorachain across Loch Monar. Look out for ravens playing on the wind and, if you are lucky, a golden eagle. Gradually the angle of the path eases and it curves round to the left to enter the corrie, Toll an Lochain. Follow it until it vanishes in a peat bog. There are a couple of small cairns to mark the end of the path. Try to take note of this place, as you will need to return to it. From here strike out to your right, bearing almost due south and picking a careful route through the peat hags to reach a ridge of higher ground along the middle of the corrie which gives easier walking and from where you can see both lochans. Aim for the col between An Riabhachan to the right and Sgurr na Lapaich to the left, to look for the hidden lochan, Loch Mòr, tucked away at the back of the corrie This is most attractive, nestling below the steep back wall of the corrie, and where you might see black-throated divers in summer. Its partner, Loch Beag, to the right, is equally delightful and hides below an impressive double buttress on the ridge from An Riabhachan.

3 When you have explored the corrie make your way back to the lip, looking carefully for the place where the path emerges from the bog, to retrace your steps to the parking area. If you miss the start of the path, just make your way down over the lip on steeper ground; the zigzags of the path here are obvious.

Black-throated diver

Practicals

Type of walk: Choose a good day for this dramatic walk, preferably during a spell of dry weather. It is on good tracks and paths except for the corrie, which is pathless and rough. Care needs to be taken to find the path down from it. It is a very remote and unfrequented area and you need to go well equipped.

Complete distance: 7 miles/11.5km
Time: 4–5 hours to give time for exploration
Maps: OS Explorer 430/Landranger 25

15

Sgurr Fhuar-thuill and
Sgurr na Fearstaig

Park about a mile beyond Braulen Lodge on the right where a track goes off. There is plenty of space at the beginning of the track, grid ref 224392. To access this, drive along the private road from Struy in Strathglass up Glen Strathfarrar. There is a locked gate across the road at Inchmore, ¼ mile/0.5 km west of Struy Bridge. The gatekeeper, who lives in the cottage beside the gate, will open it for you between 9am and 5pm from April to the end of October, except on Tuesdays all day or Wednesday mornings till 13.30. Exit time varies with day length but can be up to 8pm in June, July and August. In winter (November to March) the gate is left open at present (see previous walk).

Glen Strathfarrar is the most northerly of the three long glens, which run eastward to Strathglass. Its watershed is only 15 miles/28km from the west coast. The lower part of the glen is a National Nature Reserve and the long drive up to the Monar Dam glen is a delight, through magnificent native birch and pine woodland and past two small lochs.

Loch Toll a'Mhuic

53

The ridge on the north side of Glen Strathfarrar has four Munros and two tops, and the whole traverse forms a fine day's walk. The only disadvantage is that the start and finish are 3¾/6km miles apart. This walk avoids the road walking by climbing only **Sgurr Fhuar-thuill** and the top of Sgurr na Fearstaig which are the finest peaks in the group, and the return over Sgurr na Muice gives the best views.

1 Walk up the track with the Allt Toll a' Mhuic surging below to your right. Look for butterfly and fragrant orchids in June and July. The track climbs steadily and after about ½ mile/1 km becomes a good stalkers' path, still beside the burn. Higher up the corrie look for a path joining from the left, which is your return route. Shortly after this the path crosses the Allt Toll a' Mhuic on stones and runs along the far side. As it climbs you can see Loch Toll a' Mhuic to your left, cradled below the crags of Sgurr na Muice; you may see red-throated divers on it in summer.

2 The path is rather indistinct in places in the grassy corrie above the lochan, but it can be clearly seen ahead where it ascends the headwall of the corrie. It climbs gently across the steep slope to reach the ridge between Sgurr na Fearstaig and Sgurr Fhuar-thuill. Turn right along this ridge with a spectacular drop into the northern corrie, and climb to the summit of Sgurr Fhuar-thuill. Enjoy the splendid view. This is the first Munro of the group known as the 'Strathfarrar Four'.

3 Then retrace your steps along the ridge past the path you came up. The ridge becomes quite narrow and rocky but is nowhere difficult. The summit of Sgurr na Fearstaig is soon reached. Carry on down the grassy slopes beyond the summit, listening for the plaintive piping of golden plovers,

Red-throated diver

and follow the ridge which runs southwards to Sgurr na Muice. (If you wish to descend quickly there is a short steep grassy slope leading down to the stalkers' path you came up.) Climb Sgurr na Muice; there is a magnificent view westward from this ridge along Loch Monar to the remote mountains at its head. Go west for about 165ft/50m from the summit to avoid the cliffs above Loch Toll a'Mhuic and then make your way down steeply southwards over rather broken rocky ground to the col between Sgurr na Muice and Carn an Daimh Bhain, then turn left to follow a stalkers' path running below the crags. Where you meet the main path, turn right and return down by the burn to the road and your car.

Fragrant and Lesser Butterfly Orchids

Practicals

Type of walk: An excellent climb up a good path in fairly remote country. All the usual precautions for climbing Munros should be taken.

Complete distance: 9 miles/14.5km
Time: 5–6 hours
Maps: OS Explorer 430/Landranger 25

16

Meall Fuar-mhonaidh

Park in the car park near the end of the surfaced road between Balbeg and Grotaig, grid reference 492239. To reach this turn right off the A82 at the east end Borlum Bridge at Lewiston, south of Drumnadrochit, signposted to Bunloit (Bun Leothaid). This minor road climbs steeply with hairpin bends until it levels out at the top of the bank and thereafter runs fairly straight along a ridge. There is a footpath for the Great Glen Way beside it in places.

Meall Fuar-mhonaidh (Meall Fuarvonie) is the prominent hill on the north-west side of Loch Ness. At 2297ft/699m it does not quite reach Corbett status, but because of its position it provides magnificent views along the whole length of the Great Glen and is a popular tourist climb. It also has the distinction of being the highest hill in the country composed of the Old Red Sandstone, although the upper part is actually a coarse conglomerate full of pebbles.

Meall Fuar-mhonaidh

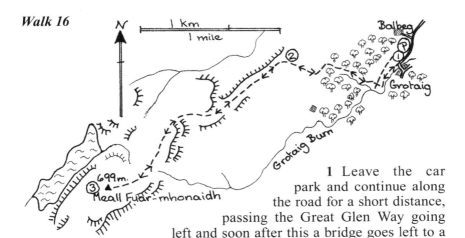

Walk 16

1 Leave the car park and continue along the road for a short distance, passing the Great Glen Way going left and soon after this a bridge goes left to a Pottery. Then take a gated path on the right, signed 'Hill Path'. Go on along by a burn through trees, to a gate leading into an open area where the ground is wet and at the right time of year is carpeted with ragged robin, valerian and meadowsweet. Listen here for the churring of a grasshopper warbler. Then carry on into mixed deciduous woodland. There is a burn to your left. Cross a track with a gate at each side and climb steeply through the woodland following waymarks. Beyond a section of duckboarding, go through another gate then on up through birch woodland and eventually out on to the open fell. Climb fairly steeply up the obvious path to a ladder stile over a deer fence. A notice here states that shooting takes place from mid-August to mid-February and in this period you are asked to stay on the path.

2 Carry on up to a long ridge leading towards the dominant peak ahead. The going is quite good along the ridge, relatively dry and stony, and the views down to Loch Ness are fine. Continue climbing up the distinct path, which spreads rather in boggy places and you will have to pick your way. Look out for mountain hares. As you

Mountain hare

57

approach the summit the way becomes steeper but is nowhere difficult. After reaching a cairn, go downhill a little and climb the last pull up to the rocky top and the final cairn. The view from here is splendid, with the whole of the Great Glen laid out before you, and to the west the hills around Glens Affric, Cannich and Strathfarrar. The moorland below is studded with lochans, and even at this distance you may hear the weird wild call of red-throated divers which nest there.

3 Retrace your outward path back to the car park.

Cloudberry

Practicals

Type of walk: A very enjoyable climb with a distinct path all the way. It can be wet in places and requires good footwear, but the views provide an excellent reward for the effort.

Complete distance: 6 miles/9.5km

Time: 4–5 hours

Maps: OS Explorer 416/Landranger 26

17

Craigmonie and Divach Falls

Park by the Tourist Information Centre in Drumnadrochit, grid ref 508299. Access this along the A82 from Inverness to Fort Augustus, on the north-west side of Loch Ness.

Falls of Divach

Falls of Divach, sometimes known as Loch Ness-side falls, are well worth visiting.They are some 100ft/31m high and embowered in trees. They have inspired writers and artists. A painting of the Falls by John Phillips hangs in Buckingham Palace. They brought the first tourists to the area. Visitors would arrive by boat at Temple Pier and then be taken to the Falls. The woods are managed by the Forestry Commission and the Woodland Trust.

A legend tells that in the 11th century Norsemen were defeated in a battle with the local people. One of the invaders, a **Scandinavian Prince known as Monie**, fled with his sister from the battle scene and hid on Craig Monie before fleeing up Glen Urquhart. They were overtaken at Corriemony where Monie was slain.

Walk 17

1 Walk south along the main road from the car park, to turn right into Pitkerrald Road. Go past the entrance to the school and take the next left turn, signed to Craigmonie and Balmacaan Woods. Beyond the houses the road becomes a reinforced track. Continue to an information board beside a huge redwood *Sequoiadendron giganteum*. Then go on along the pleasant track through mixed deciduous woodland; this was once the drive to Balmacaan House. Beyond a bungalow, the track slopes downhill and houses start again; turn right before you reach them along a track with a high wall to the left and woods to the right. Go right past a house called the Wash House, then fork left and almost immediately take a small path on the right which runs steeply uphill to the top of a bank. Bear left onto a delightful path at the top, which runs through open oak woodland with kettleholes (see walk 21) below on either side. You might see spotted flycatchers, long-tailed tits, bullfinches and treecreepers.

2 Take the left branch at the next T-junction for the Divach Falls. Go through a small wicket gate and turn left, then right onto a larger track. Pass a bungalow on the right and descend gently to turn left at the next junction. At the road ahead turn right, following a sign for the Falls. The very minor road runs through more lovely oak woodland, crosses the burn and then climbs steeply up the far side out into open fields. Turn sharply right where two tracks go off, and admire the view back down the glen to Loch Ness. There is a small car park on the right and at its end a gate gives access to a path down through the wood to a viewpoint for the fine waterfall.

3 Return to the road and retrace your steps to the place where you joined it. Go back the way you came, up the forest track for 132ft/45m then

60

right to pass the bungalow. Turn left before the next bungalow and go through the wicket gate again into the wood. Keep left at the next path junction, then go left again down the slope to cross a track and climb the path at the far side. Keep inside the woodland, but not far from the edge. Join a path coming up from the right and then walk between two mounds of stones.

4 Shortly after these take a small path on the right, which, in a few yards, leads to another path. Turn left and climb the slope, round crags, and then out to a fine viewpoint overlooking Drumnadrochit

Spotted flycatcher

and Loch Ness; there is a seat here. This rocky promontory is the Craig Monie of the legend, and you can make out the remains of a dun or fort on the highest point. Continue round the top on a good path between fine old pine trees. Bear right to join the path along the edge of the wood and follow this down to a cross of paths where the field on the left comes to an end. Turn left here to walk along the top of the wood below the field.

5 The path winds down into conifers. Look for the path to a viewpoint on the right, then continue downwards along the bottom of the wood. There are many glimpses out over the pleasant valley. A path joins from the right and then another. Keep left and eventually go downhill to come out at the side of the enormous redwood mentioned earlier. Turn left and retrace your steps into Drumnadrochit to return to your car.

Practicals

Type of walk: Pleasantly wooded with some fine views. Good tracks and paths and a section of quiet road.

Complete distance: 5 miles/8km

Time: 3 hours

Maps: OS Explorer 416/Landranger 26

18

Abriachan Woods and Carn na Leitire

Park in the car park of the Abriachan Forest Trust, grid ref 542355. To reach this drive south along the A82 from Inverness towards Fort William. About 3 miles after the start of Loch Ness look for signs to Abriachan and drive up the steep road on the right, through the township. Bear left at a Y-junction and carry on past Loch Laide. The car park lies along a left turn 443yds/400m ahead.

Abriachan Forest Trust owns and manages this area and provides and maintains the excellent footpath network. Their woods join an area of deciduous woodland managed by the Woodland Trust down by the shore of Loch Ness. Their aims are to increase the mixed native woodland and so to enhance the biodiversity and attractiveness of the area, and to ensure continued public access, providing enjoyment, educational facilities and jobs.

The Shieling, Abriachan

The Great Glen runs along the line of a geological fault, which cuts Scotland in two. Rocks to the north west bear no relation to those to the south east. During the Ice Age the line of the fault provided a route for glaciers, which gouged out the U-shaped valley containing Lochs Ness, Oich, Lochy and Linnhe.

Shielings were small huts where the people lived whilst they were up in the hills tending their animals at the summer grazings.

1 Cross to the far side of the car park and take a path beside an information board. Turn right near a tree house and follow the path as it winds left. Continue through dense forest to an open space with a thatched hut. Turn left at the next cross of tracks. At a fork go left, winding round the hillside with trees to your right. Climb steeply through an open area with scattered birch and juniper, to a carved wooden bench with an otter and a fish, and a lapwing and curlew on the back.

2 Go back into woodland where ferns and wood sorrel festoon the banks. Beyond the trees the path zigzags up to the top of the hill where the gradient eases. At a signpost by another carved seat turn left to Carn na Leitire. Carry on round the side of the hill and then up and down along the top of the indistinct ridge. There is a viewpoint loop off to the left. At the next fork turn left up to the cairn at the summit. Enjoy the panoramic views over Loch Laide, Ben Wyvis, Strathfarrar and the Monadhliath. Retrace your steps a short way and turn left. At a signpost, take the left

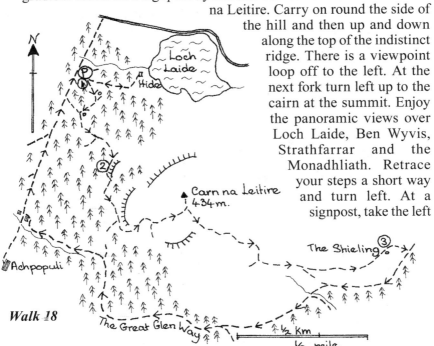

Walk 18

turn to Balchraggan. You may see stonechats and both red and black grouse. Go on over moorland with scattered Scots pines and a fine view down into the trough of the Great Glen to Loch Ness.

Stonechat

3 Come down to the Shieling which is a little heather-thatched hut, with a fantastic view down over Loch Ness and out to the Moray Firth. It is lovely and cosy inside and a good place to stop for a break. Carry on the path downhill until you reach the forest road where you turn right. Continue along this track ignoring turns to left and right until you reach the Great Glen Way and turn right. Look for roe deer and fox prints in mud or if there is snow on the ground. Wind down through the trees to meet a track coming in from the left from a house. Turn right and follow this track all the way back to the car park, bearing right when another track joins from the left. Turn right into the car park.

Woodsorrel and Feather Moss

Practicals

Type of walk: Good paths throughout, many surfaced with gravel, and some forest tracks. There is a little climbing to the top of Carn na Leitire.

Complete distance: 4 miles/6.5km

Time: 2–3 hours

Maps: OS Explorers 416 and 431/Landranger 26

19

Inverfarigaig and the Falls of Foyers

Park in the forestry car park on the right at Inverfarigaig, where there are toilets and maps giving information about the walks, grid ref 522238. To reach this, take the B852 running south-west from Inverness along the south-east shore of Loch Ness. About 8 miles/13km beyond Dores cross the River Farigaig and turn left up a minor road for 110yds/100m.

The **Falls of Foyers** were proclaimed in 1832 as not 'one of the highest cataracts in the world' but that it had a savage beauty'. Before access was made comparatively safe it was considered to be dangerous and frightening. In 1837 Joseph Mitchell, a pupil of Telford, started on plans to construct a path. Later water was extracted or diverted to power various works. In 1948 Seton Gordon commented 'Although Foyers has changed greatly during the past 25 years the scene at the great fall itself has lost nothing of its dignity and grandeur'.

A **legend** told of many waterfalls has also been attributed to Foyers. It is said that before a bridge was thrown across the ravine a tree trunk was used. One stormy night a very drunken man rode over it on horseback, safely and in great glee. Next day he went to see what he had done and when he saw the great cleft and the 'bridge' he was so appalled at his stupidity that he had a heart attack and died.

1 Walk out of the car park entrance and back down the road to the junction with the B852. Turn left and 110yds/100m further on take a right turn down towards the shore of Loch Ness. Go past several cottages on a metalled track and take a less obvious track on the right which has a blue waymark post. Continue along this delightful path, round a gate and into coniferous woodland, with birches below and views of the loch. Cross a small burn and turn left. The path climbs beside the burn,

then at a fence round an electricity complex turns left and zigzags up to a very minor road to a power station. Turn right down this road until the power station comes into view. Look for a waymark on the left and a small path climbing through the lovely oak and hazel woodland. Woodrush carpets the ground and the bushes are hung with honeysuckle. The path climbs gradually and then reaches a fence; cross a stile and climb a flight of steps to the B852. Bear right, walk past the Foyers Hotel and 110yds/100m further on take a waymarked footpath on the right descending steps and then a long sloping terrace towards the shore. Below is Foyers Bay and in winter and early spring it can be a good place to see goldeneye with tufted ducks and goosanders. You may also hear the eerie call of a diver.

2 At the end of the path ignore a flight of steps down to a road; instead carry on to join a road as it climbs the hill. Continue along it to a wider road where you turn right, then left onto a metalled track, which goes uphill, signed to Foyers Bay House and the Falls of Foyers. Just before the house

Lower Falls of Foyers

turn right onto a footpath signed to the falls and
continue along this, with a good new stout fence
to your right, above the magnificent gorge.
Look towards the loch to see a splendid bridge. Carry on up to a viewing
area, and several seats, from where
you get your first distant view of
the fine Lower Fall. Continue
climbing with the fence to your
right. Several paths go off into
the lovely mature pine woods
but ignore these. Take a
path going right, signed
for the Falls, and contour
the fenced precipitous
slope to a junction.
Here take the right
branch to a large
white boulder,
where the

Walk 19

upper viewpoint
is a few steps to the left
and from where there is a
splendid view. If you go
right you can continue down
the stepped way to the lower viewpoint.
Then climb back up again to the junction.
Turn right and ascend many more steps to
the road opposite the Foyers Stores and Post
Office, beside which is the Red Squirrel Café,
which you may like to visit.

3 If not in need of sustenance remain below
the road on a path signed to Lower Foyers.
This path runs through the wood with the road
above to your right. Take a right turn, then just before a cottage leave
the path and go up steps to the road. Turn left and walk down the
pavement, first on one side and then the other, then on the verge,
until you reach a small road on the right signed to Foyers Primary
School. Above on a knoll is a small attractive church. Walk up the
road and opposite the church turn right onto a forest track signed

to Inverfarigaig and Boleskine. This pleasant track climbs gently through the trees until you reach a level road, once tarred, where you turn left. Go past an old adit for the waterworks and continue climbing. Round a hairpin bend then almost immediately look for a small waymarked path going left. This runs down and crosses a burn then climbs up a rocky, 'knolly' hill, Toman Tarsuinn, covered with heather and young birch and scattered conifers. The path winds among the boulders until you reach a splendid viewpoint on a cluster of granite blocks.

Pine marten

4 Soon the path begins to descend again, winding in a contorted way along the ridge. At one point it seems to vanish but goes over a groove in the rock and reappears on the far side. Then it goes steeply down into dense conifers. At a waymark look carefully for the next one which is directly below; in low light it is very dark in here and there could be some confusion. Once down, emerge into open ground and cross a small valley to join a larger path on the far side. The path gets wider and more distinct as you go down, eventually turning into a clear forest track which comes out of the trees briefly near Boleskine. Turn right on a larger track and continue straight ahead, ignoring turns. At a Y-junction take the right (straight on) branch. Then wherever there is a choice go downhill. The track runs into huge trees then comes to a bridge over a burn. Do not cross but walk down with the burn to your right and down steps into the car park.

Practicals

Type of walk: A lovely walk with fine views of Loch Ness and Meall Fuar-mhonaidh, and the hills around Strathnairn. The waterfalls are spectacular. The paths are mostly good and are well waymarked but the little path over Toman Tarsuinn can be difficult to follow in places; you just have to be confident and carry on.

Complete distance: 7½ miles/12km
Time: 3–4 hours
Maps: OS Explorer 416/Landranger 26

20

Loch Duntelchaig to Loch Ruthven

Park in the long layby at the north east end of Loch Duntelchaig, just before the entrance to the waterworks, grid reference 647321. To reach this, leave the A9 along the B851 to Fort Augustus and turn right for Dunlichity Trout Farm. Follow the road round past Loch a'Chlachain. If you are using two cars for this walk the second one should park in the RSPB car park at Loch Ruthven, signed from the B851, grid reference 638281.

This walk can be done with two cars and may be done from either end. Or you may wish to walk both ways. Beautiful tranquil **Loch Ruthven** is fringed with birch woodland and sedges, the latter the haunt of toads. Visit in early spring to see the Slavonian grebes, colourful in full breeding plumage. The loch is the most important breeding site for these rare birds and it has one of the highest populations of this species in Europe. The reserve has no toilets or catering facilities.

1 Walk on from the car park and turn left down the road belonging to Scottish Water, where there are Walkers Welcome signs. Go past the works and on along a track round the loch above the shoreline. The woods are beautiful with birch and rowan. After a short while the

Loch Ruthven

Walk 20

Loch
Duntelchaig

Stac
an
Fhithich

½ km
½ mile

N

Loch
a'Choire

Loch
Ruthven

Hide
(RSPB)

track begins to climb and there is a spectacular crag, much used by climbers, on the left. Then the path runs into conifer woodland. Soon there is a clear-felled area on the right, from where there are fine views over the loch and you might see buzzards and maybe a peregrine. Carry on to a cottage with a pleasant garden overlooking the loch. After this the path rises gradually through more clear-fell, then enters the trees again. Ignore a right turn and zigzag upwards, eventually reaching the summit in an open heathery area.

2 Descend again into the trees. Wind round above the steep slope down to Loch a'Choire, enjoying the view of it through the trees. Ignore two indistinct rides each of which is signed with a green arrow. Remain on the main track. At a junction, bear right downhill, until eventually the path levels out and runs into an open heathery area, with Loch a'Choire nearby on the right. Look for a little path, which runs through the heather to the loch shore where there is a sandy beach, a lovely place for a break. The loch is fringed with water lobelia. If you have patience and a good pair of binoculars you may see a pair of Slavonian grebes, and maybe a heron.

3 Return to the track and continue down to the road. Cross the stile and turn left. Loch Ruthven is down to the right, set among steep craggy hills. Go past some houses and downhill to a car park. (Maybe you will be met here.) Pass through the car park, past the RSPB sign, and on down a narrow path to the loch. Here a narrow path leads to a rocky breakwater where you may see grebes. Then go on along the path, with boardwalks over the wet areas, through the delightful

birchwood, winding along above the loch to cross a small burn and go up to a hide. The hide overlooks a reedy area the place, in spring and early summer, to spot the grebes. Also look for ospreys, which often fish here.

4 Return to the car park, then if necessary walk back along your outward route to the start, enjoying all the views missed earlier.

Slavonian grebe

Birch

Practicals

Type of walk: Straightforward, along forestry tracks, with a lovely path to the RSPB hide at the end. Good views and good birdwatching.

Complete distance: 5 miles/8km one way
Time: 3 hours one way
Maps: OS Explores 416 and 417/Landranger 26

21

The Inverarnan Esker Trail, Littlemill Forest

Park in the forestry car park by the gate, two miles along the road from the junction with the A9, grid ref 701366. Access this along the B851 which leaves the A9 about 1½ miles/2.5km south of Daviot.

Eskers are ridges formed during the last ice age as riverbeds, by rivers flowing in channels under the ice. They deposited sand, gravel and boulders. When the ice melted they were left as ridges above the surrounding countryside.

Kettleholes are deep depressions, often with lochans in, which formed where a block of ice was left in the moraine as the bulk of the ice melted. When they finally melted they left a hole.

Glacial erratics are boulders which were carried by the ice far from their place of origin. There are several along this walk.

Kettlehole Lochan

1 Go round the barrier gate and walk straight ahead up the track. Soon it begins to climb steeply up a bank, which is in fact the side of an esker. At the top turn left following blue waymarkers and climb some more to walk along the top of a long curving esker. Soon an attractive kettlehole lochan comes into view on the right.

2 Carry on along the ridge with twisted pines to your left until you reach the sand and gravel quarry boundary. At a waymark descend steeply from the esker and keep along the good path by the fence. This leads into birch and then pine woodland and climbs until you are walking along a ride on top of a lower esker. Come out into an open area where there is a path junction and turn left, following red waymarks. Then climb steps and a steep slope to the top of a higher ridge and walk through the lovely open area with a large kettlehole lochan to your right where you may see goldeneye. There is a splendid view to the hills round Strathnairn. Continue beyond the lochan until you come down gently to a gap. There is a fork in the path here with a clear branch running left but take the right way-marked one. This soon winds left and slants up gradually and not very clearly through a birchwood.

3 At the top, at another waymark, cross over a bank onto a good path running along the ridge. This path continues for a long way with a rampart to the right and pines sloping down to a burn on the left. The red marked path goes right but keep on along the top of the esker now following yellow markers. Then descend gently and turn left across a clear-felled area to climb a bank and go down into the flat floor of an old gravel pit. If you look at the sides you will find places where there are sections through the eskers, showing the mixed up sand, gravel and boulders. Keep to the right side and leave the gravel pit by a good clear track which takes you to a gate into a young plantation.

Walk 21

73

4 Turn right before the gate onto another track and follow it for about half a mile to a junction. Look here for glacial erratics. Turn left on a new path. It bends right and then left again, then winds up the side of another esker which runs along above a very shallow lochan and then above the large lochan seen earlier. Climb steeply to a seat, then turn left and go down again and round above another hole with the remains of a lochan in it. Soon the path joins a larger track where you turn left and retrace your outward steps to your car.

Goldeneye

Practicals

Type of walk: Interesting with good views and clear paths throughout

Complete distance: 3 miles/5km
Time: 2–3 hours
Maps: OS Explorer 416/Landranger 27 and 26

22

Nairn to Cawdor along River Nairn

Park in the large car park called the Maggot at the end of the road by the harbour bridge (now for pedestrians only), grid ref 889571. Access this along the A96 from Inverness. Cross the bridge over the River Nairn and turn left.

This is **not a circular walk** and when you reach Cawdor you have the choice of returning by the same route or catching a bus back to the start. Highland Country bus, number 12, travels from Inverness and on to Nairn and then Cawdor.

Nairn is an ancient fishing port and market town. The harbour was constructed by Thomas Telford. Nairn hosts one of the biggest Highland games in the north, the first event being held in 1867.

On your walk, look out for **dippers**. They are rotund, short-tailed birds, dark above and white breasted. You might spot one on a rock, mid stream, bobbing in spasmodic

*Cawdor
Castle*

curtsies. It dives and walks into the water, deliberately submerging to the bottom after larvae of aquatic insects. It has a sweet, hurried song mainly heard from December until May. Its nest is generally constructed above water in grooves in rocks or in small holes under bridges.

Walk 22

1 Cross the harbour bridge and explore the harbour, then return. Turn right at the far side along a paved pathway, signed 'Riverside Walk to Cawdor'. There is a green space called the 'Maggot' on the left and the River Nairn to your right. Go under the road bridge on a raised pathway, cross another grassy area and walk under the left arch of a magnificent railway viaduct. Carry on past the Jubilee Footbridge and then where the tarred path bears left, continue along the riverbank on a reinforced path. The river is lovely here, swift flowing with trees on both banks. Keep a lookout here for goosanders.

2 Walk past the Firhill footbridge. Then the path becomes a little less park-like although it is still well made. After some distance it climbs the bank with steps in places and narrows considerably to run along beside the field fence, with a steep, wooded drop down to the river in its gorge below. Take care on this section as the path is quite narrow, muddy and slippery in places. Then go down to the riverside where there is a flat area, and soon back up the bank to come out at a layby by Howford bridge.

3 Cross the main road and take the signed path, which runs along beside it. Soon this goes downhill through Scots pine and beech to a wooden

footbridge over the Geddes Burn at the bottom. Then carry on along the floodplain of the river, which here is wide and braided with many trees carried down in floods. The path runs through sycamore and alder woods, where you might see long-tailed tits. Where it comes near to the riverbank look for roe deer, dippers and more goosanders. There is a grassy clearing with a bench and a memorial above a lovely pool in the river. The path goes down very close to the water and soon

Dipper

climbs up again onto a flood-bank. At first this runs through alders but then comes out into broom. In winter this part of the walk can be rather bleak but in summer when the broom is in flower it is transformed. There are pleasant views out across the fields to the hills.

4 Eventually the path leaves the flood-bank and winds down through the broom and into trees again. Go through a kissing gate and along the river bank. Look for dippers and you may also see a heron. The path runs between gorse bushes and then along the edge of a plantation of Douglas fir, followed by a wood of mature pines with scattered deciduous trees. Follow the waymarks right to return to the river, which soon divides; the path goes left beside the Cawdor Burn. Ignore the waymarks indicating left and carry on beside the burn to the road bridge. Turn left then right for the castle, open from May to mid-October, or right into the village where there is an excellent inn, the Cawdor Tavern. The castle also has an extremely good restaurant and is very interesting to visit, and there are some splendid nature trails in the beautiful woods behind the castle. Unfortunately this is where this walk ends. Here you must decide whether to retrace your path to Nairn, or return by bus.

Practicals

Type of walk: On good paths beside a pleasing river.

Complete distance: 5 miles/8km one way, 10 miles/16km if you do both ways

Time: 3 or 6 hours

Maps: OS Explorer 422/Landranger 27

23a

Cawdor Forest

Park on the side of the road close to where the path goes down to Greystone Bridge, grid ref 840490, taking care not to block passing places or forest entrances. To access this drive along the A96 eastwards from Inverness, then turn right onto the B9090 to Cawdor. Take a right turn onto a minor road at the beginning of the village and drive along it for ½ mile/0.5km.

Greystone Bridge

Cawdor Castle was established as a fortified tower house towards the second half of the 14th century. It is privately inhabited and the Thanes of Cawdor have lived in the castle continuously for 600 years. It has had some grisly happenings in the past. Both the 4th and the 11th Thanes were brutally murdered. Another story told is that when she was a baby, the mother of one of the Thanes was branded by her own mother so that nobody could impersonate her.

Walk 23a

1 Go round a barrier and take the good track down through the mature deciduous woodland to Greystone Bridge. Cross and walk ahead on the clear track. Look right for the huge boulder, the Grey Stone, which gives the bridge its name. Where two paths branch off the track on the right, take the farthest right which leads back towards the river, the Allt Dubh, and follow it along the river bank and up onto the river terrace through magnificent beech woodland. In places the huge trees look like the pillars of a cathedral. The river comes nearer again and runs in a gorge with little waterfalls. On the far side is a house perched precariously above the cliff. Climb steeply up the bank and then wind round with the river far below to come to a path junction.

2 Turn left and walk down a wide track through oak woodland, then beneath superb huge larch trees. Look for red squirrels feeding on the cones; and you may see bullfinches or hear a song thrush singing. The ground is carpeted with greater woodrush. Ignore a grassy path going left, then two tracks on the right, then another path on the left. Keep to the main path as it goes steadily downhill back into ancient oak wood. It bends right and descends to the Riereach Burn at the New Bridge. You are asked not to take animals, unsupervised children or unauthorised vehicles across, nor to swing on the railings.

3 At the far side walk ahead for a few steps then turn left through a rhododendron thicket on a small path. This soon emerges into open

woodland and then runs just below the top of a bank with a fence and a field above, with a huge magnificent redwood on the left. The path then dives through another thicket of contorted rhododendrons and winds right. Look for a small path going left down to the river and cross on a narrow wooden bridge, built by the army in 1986. Turn right at the far side and walk down to the confluence of the two burns where there is a fine pool, then bear left along the high bank of the Allt Dearg. The river winds in tight meanders with sandy banks and rapids. Continue on the path into open beech woodland once more. Keep ahead until the way joins a track; turn right to recross Greystone Bridge and return to your car.

Bullfinch

Practicals

Type of walk: A delightful walk on pleasant well-maintained paths through magnificent woodland.

Complete distance: 2 1/2 miles/4 km

Time: 1–2 hours

Maps: OS Explorer 422/Landranger 27

NB After your walk you may like to visit Cawdor Castle where there are fine gardens as well as the castle itself, and an excellent tearoom. Whilst in the area you may find time to visit the superb chambered cairns, known as the **Clava Cairns** – see the next walk 23b.

23b

Balnuaran of Clava

Park in the car park on the right 325yds/300m along this road, grid ref 768445. To reach this from Cawdor, return along the B9090 to Clephanton and turn left onto the B9006 to Croy and Culloden. Go left on the B851 into Leanach and then immediately left again. Cross the River Nairn and turn right. There are signs to Clava Cairns at all the nearby road junctions.

Balnuaran of Clava is the site of an exceptionally well preserved group of prehistoric burial cairns. It is believed that about 2,000BC a row of large cairns was built, three of which can be seen today. A short way along the road, through the valley, at Milton of Clava, are traces of a smaller cemetery. The cairns were built along a gravel terrace raised above the River Nairn. No traces of the bodies placed in the cairns survive.

1 From the car park walk through the kissing gate into the delightful site where scattered mature trees shade the cemetery. Here there are the

Chambered Cairn, Clava

three large cairns and one small one; you will want to spend some time exploring, viewing the standing stones and reading the informative boards.

2 Leave the peaceful area through a small gate at the far end and walk along the minor road to a right-angled bend. Continue straight ahead on a fenced path through fields until you reach an enclosure at Milton of Clava. The cairn here is not so well preserved, but there is also an enclosure containing the remnants of a medieval chapel.

3 On your return to the parking area enjoy the splendid view back down Strathnairn to the red sandstone railway viaduct over the River Nairn.

Walk 23b

Siskin

Practicals

Type of walk: Short and level. A pleasing step back 4000 years.

Complete distance: 1 mile/1.5km

Time: 1 hour

Maps: OS Explorer 422/Landranger 27

NB After your visit to the Cairns you might wish to visit the site of the Culloden Battlefield, grid ref 740448.

24

Craig Phadrig and the Caledonian Canal

Park in the large car park by the canal at Dochgarroch, grid ref 618405. To reach this, take the A82 Inverness to Fort William road. About 4 miles/6.5km south of Inverness look for an entry to the Oakwood Restaurant and Dochgarroch and drive along the track to the car park where there are toilets.

Craig Phadrig is the site of an iron-age hillfort, dating from around 500BC. It was still occupied in 565AD when St.Columba possibly met King Brude of the Picts here, and converted him to Christianity. The fort itself is an example of a vitrified fort, where the stone walls have been fused together by great heat, though whether by accident or on purpose no-one knows.

Locks, Caledonian Canal

The Caledonian Canal links a series of lochs running along the fault line of the Great Glen. It was completed in 1822, as part of a project to open up the Highlands in the aftermath of the Jacobite Rebellions. The engineer was Thomas Telford. It provided shelter for the Navy from French privateers. It became a success for commercial craft from 1880 on. Now it is used only by fishing boats and leisure craft, providing an easier and quicker journey from west to east coasts. It is 60 miles/99km long with 22 miles/34km canalised, the rest being open lochs. It has 22 locks, including the splendid flight at Banavie, which is called Neptune's Staircase. The highest point is Loch Oich at 106 ft/33m above sea level.

1 Walk out of the car park in the direction of Inverness. Go round a barrier at the end of the tarmac and on along the track, with boats moored on your right. At the end of the track follow a sign directing you right along the delightful grassy canal path. Go past a cottage on the left and through a gate, then round a locked metal gate and almost immediately take a small path on the left. Climb through a wood of young Scots pines surrounding the remains of an iron-age hill fort. Where the path forks, go left into more mature woodland and then along the edge of the wood with a field to the left to come out onto the A82.

2 Cross with extreme care, turn right and walk along the grassy verge for 20yds/18m then turn left where there is a sign for Inverness Crematorium and Kilvean Cemetery and a footpath sign. Continue up the metalled road past the Cemetery car park, and take the waymarked path which goes straight on. It becomes a delightful wooded lane along the hillside, then bends sharply right and goes past a ruined building with towers and crenellations, once a hospital which burnt down, and then the headquarters of SNH. Turn left up the road out of the complex, following signs for the Great Glen Way. Enjoy the fantastic view over Inverness and the Moray Firth, and keep a look out for red kites. At a T-junction turn left along the Great Glen Way. Follow it as it winds right through a wood to the top of the hill. Go round a fenced reservoir, through a wicket gate and turn right onto a track. Join another track where the Great Glen Way goes left, but this walk turns right, through birch, pine and gorse with a stone wall on the left. Beyond a house the track joins a metalled road where you walk straight ahead.

3 Ignore a turn on the left and carry on to the car park for Craig Phadrig. Walk through the car park and round the gate at the end. Carry on along

the track for about 110yds/100m, take an acute turn back on the right, and almost immediately turn left. Cross a burn and begin to climb. At a T- junction turn right, then right again at a way-marker. The path veers left and climbs steeply up steps through pine and beech. Go left again up a steep slope to the top of the hill fort and walk round the rampart. The fort is large and impressive. There are glimpses through the trees of Inverness on one side and the Beauly Firth on the other. At the far end of the fort, descend a steep small path, which joins the circular path below the fort. Turn left, then after a short distance turn right and carry on downhill to a big turning area where the way-marked path goes left.

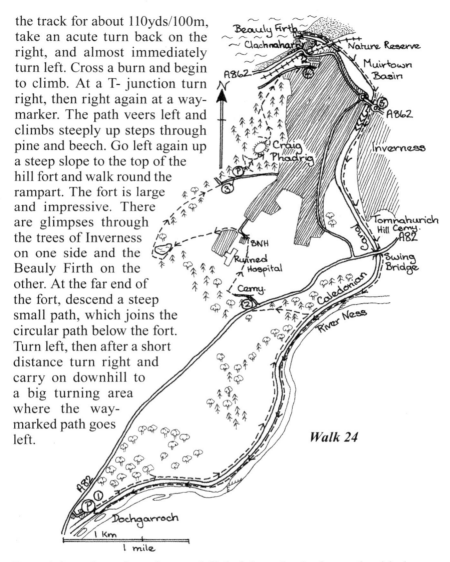

Walk 24

Bear right and continue down a delightful gently sloping path with the Beauly Firth through the trees to the left. At a minor road walk round the locked gate and turn right.

4   Beyond the first two houses, on the left, go down steps on the left to a lower road. Carry on down and turn left at the bottom to take a little path winding round the end fence of the last house and descending to

a monument. Continue down the stepped path, where you may see a red squirrel, to join the main road (A862) where it crosses the railway. Go over the bridge with great care and immediately turn right to walk through Clachnaharry. Turn left past a green area to the canal towpath where you turn left and walk down to the end. Cross the canal by the sea lock gate, enjoying the wide views over the Beauly Firth. Look for dolphins, wigeon, tufted duck, goldeneye, curlews and oystercatchers. Go along the towpath on the far side and cross the level crossing with care. Beyond another lock is the Muirtown basin, where many craft are moored.

5 Cross the very busy main road and head up the left side of the flight of four locks. Continue along the path past an attractive wooded hill with a cemetery at its base, to the swing bridge at Tomnahurich. Cross the road with care. Carry on along the towpath which is lovely with the quiet canal on the right and the River Ness foaming and rushing over a weir on the left. Watch out for kingfishers, often just a flash of brilliant blue. The boats at Dochgarroch come into view. Cross the lock gate and return to the car park.

Kingfisher

Practicals

Type of walk: A long walk all on good paths and much of it is level.

Distance: 13 miles/21km
Time: 5–6 hours
Maps: OS Explorer 416/Landranger 26

25

Reelig Glen

Park in the Forestry Commission car park where the minor road makes a hairpin bend to the left, grid ref 558431. This is accessed along the A862 from Inverness to Beauly. About 8 miles/13km out of Inverness and a mile beyond a turning on the right to Kirkhill, take a minor road on the left signed to Reelig Glen Forest Walks. Drive straight ahead following signs.

The **Glen walks** were laid out by James Baillie Fraser in the early 19th century, after the style of gardeners like Capability Brown. Many exotic trees were planted. The trees have grown very tall in the sheltered conditions of the glen.

Bridge, Reelig Glen

The Douglas fir was newly imported into Britain from western North America, having been discovered there by David Douglas. The tallest Douglas fir here, called **Dughaill Mor**, at 211ft/65m, has a claim to be the tallest tree in Scotland.

David Douglas (1798–1834) was an important botanical collector and the Douglas fir is named after him. He made heroic and often arduous explorations, collecting species from forests and gardens. Once he made an enormous journey, often on foot, between the Pacific and Hudson Bay. He died aged 35 after falling into a pit for trapping wild cattle where he was gored by a savage wild bull.

Walk 25

1 Take a path on the right out of the car park; it is way-marked but not as obvious as the one straight ahead. Climb up steps and then steep zigzags to reach a ridge above the glen. Follow the way-marks to the right to a viewpoint where you can look out over the fertile countryside. Then carry on left, climbing gently, to a flat area with an information board. Head on along the right flank of the ridge, over a small burn and up to a magnificent stand of mature beech trees, known as 'The Cathedral'. Red squirrels abound in the woods here so keep a lookout. Beyond the beeches the path runs parallel to a minor road to come to a small car park.

2 Turn left here and walk gently downhill until you reach a wider path contouring the hillside. Go left on this and wind through the pleasant woodland, with a steep drop to your right. Look for bullfinches in the trees. Cross a wooden bridge and at a waymark you can either walk straight ahead to rejoin your outward path or bear right onto a smaller path which continues along the edge of the steep slope. This eventually comes downhill to rejoin the outer path at the information board. Turn right and follow a made but unsigned path round the outer edge of a small knoll, then leave it, right, to continue down the ridge. This rejoins the outward path at the top of the steep zigzags back down to the car park.

Red Squirrel

3 Then take the other, more obvious, path out of the car park, which runs beside the Moniack Burn. This is a wheelchair path for the first ¼ mile/0.5km and is very level. The trees are superb. Then the path goes uphill, crosses a side burn and slopes downhill to a wooden footbridge over the Moniack Burn. Beside it is the original bridge, a fine stone-built packhorse bridge decorated with ferns, but fences prevent access, presumably because it is without parapets. At the far side is a grotto, with pillars and an archway made of stone to look like a ruin.

4 Cross the bridge and go along the continuing path, which winds below cliffs on the far side. Then come downhill into a grove of huge Douglas firs, one of which has a claim to be the tallest tree in Scotland, 211ft/65m when last measured. The path on this side winds as it goes uphill to follow a terrace and then down again. When you reach the road turn left, cross the bridge and go left again into the car park.

Practicals

Type of walk: Delightful short walk through some superb forestry.

Complete distance: 2 miles/3.4km

Time: 1–2 hours

Maps: OS Explorer 416/Landranger 26

26

River Beauly to Lovat Bridge

Park in the small layby on the right of the road just beyond Kiltarlity Bridge, opposite the entrance to the old churchyard, grid ref 497439. To access this turn off the A862 a mile south of Beauly onto the A831. After a mile turn left onto a minor road to Kiltarlity and cross the bridge over the River Beauly.

Beaufort Castle was built as a fortress in the late 13th century by the Frasers of Lovat. It was known as Dounie Castle. It had a turbulent history and was finally destroyed in the 18th century. After being rebuilt it was called Beaufort Castle. In the 1990s it was sold because of huge debts. It was bought by Ann Gloag, sister of Brian Souter, who together founded and built up the Stagecoach Transport Group.

About 10 miles/16km from Beauly on the River Beauly is the **Aigas fish lift**. This allows fish to by-pass the Aigas Dam. Electronic counters record the number of fish passing through them and they are able to distinguish between ascending and descending fish. It is open to the public during the summer months.

Lovat Bridge

1 Walk back across the bridge, along the pedestrian way to cross the road and go through a gate opposite. If the gate is locked, pass through a gap in the fence used by fishermen. Carry on up the track into fine mature deciduous woodland. Keep on the main track well above the river, with lovely views down and across it. At the end of the wood, go through a gate gap into open land where broom thrives. Almost at once the path forks; take the right branch which brings you out of the broom and along the edge of rough grassland towards a cottage, Cruives Lodge. Turn left along its access track and follow this beside the wide river, past a long diagonal weir, until you reach another cottage, North Lodge. Cross a track and curve round the end of the lodge to reach the riverbank, where there is a turning area for fishermen and a smart fishing hut. Across the river you can catch glimpses of the imposing Beaufort Castle.

2 Go left along the pleasant track with the surging river to your right. Where a grassy track goes off right you can follow it to keep nearer to the water or keep on the inland one. They join at a wide turning area; go inland and then right onto a small but clear path through the broom, with open fields beyond to your left. Pass through a derelict gateway and on below fine beech trees on Castle Hill. Beyond, go out into open land with more broom and walk in front of a new large white lodge. Soon after this cross a footbridge over a small burn and join a track.

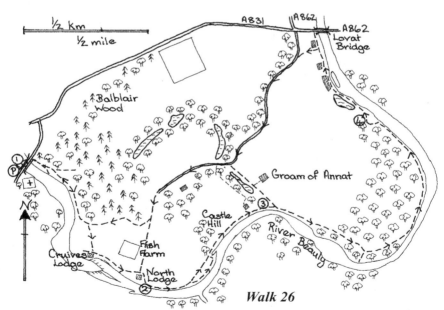

Walk 26

3 Turn right along the edge of a field to pass through a farm gate into the next field, where the cows are divided from you by an electric fence. The track becomes very clear, sandy and pleasant to walk, and it runs into deciduous woodland, mainly birch but with some oak and sycamore. Ignore a track going right towards the river. Soon the main track winds down to the river bank. You may see goldeneye and goosanders at the right time of year. In winter and early spring dippers sing from suitable stones, and if you are lucky at any time of year you may see a kingfisher. There are also signs of otters along the bank.

4 The track winds slightly left to a gate before continuing along the bank through birch and alder to a corner where it runs below a cottage. Several more bungalows follow, then in an open space there is a splendid view of Lovat Bridge, not far distant. Walk up the low river terrace and turn left in front of a converted farm building. About 165yds/150m further on turn left onto a metalled road, which passes beneath a variety of tall estate trees, with a row of limes beside it. At a T- junction turn right, cross a small burn and go uphill with a farm away to your left. Carry on through a gateway and stroll downhill. Where the road surface becomes uneven you can see the long buildings of a fish farm. Beyond the edge of a wood on the right look for a track going right and follow it round the field margin, then right uphill to keep just outside the wood. Go past a telecommunications installation on then left, soon to rejoin your outward path where it branched off through the broom. Go through the derelict gateway into the wood above the river and retrace your path to your car.

Goosander

Practicals

Type of walk: A lovely stroll on good paths and tracks with a section on a metalled road not open to most traffic.

Complete distance: 5 miles/8km

Time: 2–3 hours

Maps: OS Explorer 431/Landranger 26

NB If you have time, walk down to the old churchyard to look at the attractive ruined chapel in the shadow of a huge yew tree.

27

River Conon, Maryburgh

Park behind the Maryburgh Community Hall, opposite the Free Church of Scotland, grid ref 542565. The town is accessed by the A835 or the A862.

The quiet large village of **Maryburgh** sits on the banks of the River Conon and provides access to the historic lands of Brahan Estate. The original Brahan Castle was built in the 17th century and became the seat of the Seaforths, the principal line of the clan Mackenzie. Their estate stretched from Cromarty on the Black Isle to the Isle of Lewis. The castle was demolished in 1951 and the stone used in the foundation for the road bridge, joining Maryburgh and Conon Bridge.

Brahan estate Office

1 From the parking area walk downhill to Proby Streeet, A862, and turn right. Use the pavement on the right side of the road and stay with it as it passes through grassy areas in front of a long, narrow housing estate. Where the road bears away left to cross the railway bridge, keep ahead on the footpath and watch out, after a few steps, for a pedestrian bridge on the left that takes you over the railway. Continue on along the footpath where it comes up against the main road once more. Then when the road moves away again, keep ahead to the end of the cul-de-sac. Here take a ladderstile to go over the railway line, with care, and climb the ladderstile opposite. Turn left, as directed by a signpost, along a distinct path at the edge of a vast field, stretching up right and with the River Conon, almost hidden by vegetation, to the left.

2 Carry on along the path, which edges a wood between you and the main river, soon to arrive at the riverside once more and a footbridge over the Conon. This gives access to delightful Dunglass Island, which divides the river, where you may wish to make a mile-and-a-half circular detour before returning over the bridge and continuing, left, along the footpath. Eventually the waymarked path winds left and descends to an idyllic part of the Conon. The river is wide and stately, with grassy flats beside it, just made for your first break. Across the calm water lie pastures and Cragget wood, a dense conifer plantation. Look downstream for a flagged path that leads to a footbridge across a weir, over which pours water from the river. Here you might spot grey wagtail, whooper swan and goosander.

3 Then continue on the lovely way beside the curving river with a scattering of trees lining the banks. The path climbs steadily upwards and you

1 Km

1 mile

Maryburgh

Tallysow Wood

Brahan Estate

Dunglass Island

River Conon

N

Walk 27

94

have fine views down to the hurrying river, from *Yellowhammer* where come the whisperings of dippers. The path climbs again, higher still above the river, before leaving it to carry on along the edge of woodland, on your left. Cross a small footbridge to join a fenced footpath that continues just inside the wood and goes on until the river comes into view again. Then climb a stile into a narrow belt of woodland stretching away from the river. Bear right and rapidly, left, following the waymarks, to join a wide signposted track. It leads to a boathouse on the left, but this walk goes right, up through the splendid woodland of the Brahan estate.

4 Look left to see what was once the estate's trout pond. If you wish to visit, take a widish track left and then at the pond go right to rejoin the continuing walk. If you remain on the main track, follow it as it climbs a little, curves left and then right. There are several narrow signposted right turns off the main track and these all lead up through the old arboretum of the estate and eventually join the main track. This climbs through flower-lined banks and then passes through an area of magnificent cedar, hemlock and cypress.

5 At the T-junction, the site of the old castle, turn right to see the attractive building of the Brahan Estate Office across a field on the left. Then stroll the mile-long drive, a wide easy-to-walk track lined with superb ancient oaks for all its length. Look for tree creeper here and yellow hammer in the field to the left. Follow the wide track as it winds left with views down to Conon Bridge, Maryburgh and bulky Ben Wyvis. And then the track moves into woodland where you might spot roe deer. Keep on the main track at a skewed cross of tracks and continue with the houses of Maryburgh soon appearing to your left to descend a wide grassy track between houses on both sides. Go with the track as it curves left to join a quiet road. Turn right and then right again. Pass the church and then cross the road to reach the car park.

Practicals

Type of walk: A lovely walk, generally flat for most of the way. Good paths and tracks.

Complete distance: 6½ miles/10.5km (8 miles if you include the circuit of Dunglass Island)

Time: 3–4 hours

Maps: Landrangers 431 and 432/Landranger 26

28

Inverchoran to Glen Orrin

Park at the road end of the track down to Inverchoran; there is space to park three cars, with care, grid reference 260507. To reach this take the road from Marybank, which goes up Strathconon, and drive for 15 miles/24.6km, past Strathconon village and House.

The **River Orrin** has cut into the glacial deposits and peat that cover the floor of Glen Orrin. All about the river the glen is covered with bog and heather, with a path running above the north bank of the river used on this walk.

Loch na Frianich, Glen Orrin

1 Walk over the bridge across the River Meig, which has an alarming high cattle grid. Continue along the track towards Inverchoran. Just before you reach the fence around the house and its garden take a grassy track on the right which crosses the field to a pallisade gate. Go through and then through the next one. Turn right beside a deer fence and walk as far as the gate into a wood. Do not go through, but turn left and climb a grassy track

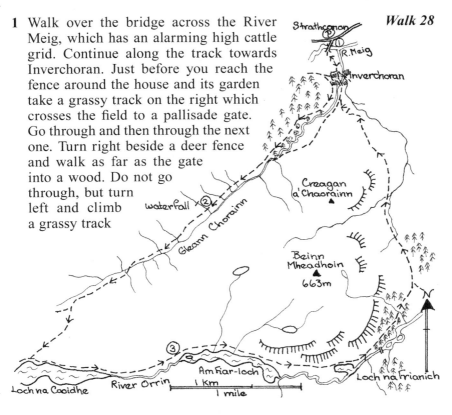

which slants up the hillside, curving round to a higher gate into the wood. Pass through this and carry on through a coniferous plantation. Whenever there is a choice of tracks keep left, along the lower edge of the trees above a fine gorge. After a while the plantation becomes pine woodland, and then the path runs out onto the open moor. Look around here for a narrow stalkers' path on which to continue up the glen, Glen Chorainn, a typical U-shaped glaciated valley. Ignore the nearby vehicle track in the bottom because it fords the river at frequent intervals.

2 About half-a-mile from where you left the wood there is a splendid waterfall on the right and the burn from this, which you need to cross, may be difficult to go over after heavy or persistent rain. Look

Emperor moth caterpillar

97

for golden-ringed and common hawker dragonflies, and maybe a snipe. Continue on the track to cross the main burn, now quite small, on stones before zigzagging up the hillside at the head of the glen where mountain saxifrage grows in wet places by the path. As you approach the col the main track keeps left and another branches off to the right, which you ignore. You may see many red deer up here. Cross the watershed and admire the fine view of Glen Orrin below and of the Strathfarrar Munros directly ahead. The path winds down into Glen Orrin to reach the valley floor halfway along Loch na Caoidhe. Turn left and follow the small path along the shore and in summer listen for common sandpipers as you go.

Opposite-leaved Golden Saxifrage

3   Walk on through Glen Orrin, past Am Fiar-Loch and then the little Loch na Frianich. At first the glen is narrow and enclosed but as you progress it opens out and the Strathfarrar hills appear again on the right, notably Carn nan Gobhar with its pointed boulder-strewn summit. Beside the path you should see both round-leaved and long-leaved sundews, butterwort and masses of bog asphodel. Look out for large heath butterflies and the green emperor moth caterpillars. Past Loch Frianich the path becomes a track beside the river, and a suspension bridge appears ahead. The track swings left up the hillside just before you reach the bridge and runs along above a fenced plantation, then enters old pine forest, where you may see roe deer and spotted fly-catchers. Climb up through the lovely old trees, with splendid cliffs above them,

Roe Deer

to emerge onto the moorland and up to the col. The track becomes more used and therefore less easy to walk but descends in tight zigzags down the far side towards Inverchoran. Turn right on the track at the bottom, cross the bridge and walk ahead between the barn and the fenced steading to come to the pallisade gates. Go through and return across the fields to your car.

*Round-leaved and
Long-leaved sundew*

Practicals

Type of walk: A good hill walk in a remote area, on clear paths and tracks. There is one burn, which might cause difficulty after rain. The final mile of track is rough and stony. In the stalking season look out for notices about access. If in doubt, call the estate office (01997 477230).

Complete distance: 10 miles/16.5km
Time: 6 hours
Maps: OS Explorer 430/Landranger 25

29

Ben Wyvis

Park in the large forestry car park, signed Ben Wyvis Car Park, on the east of the road before Garbat, grid ref 411672. Access is from the A835 Inverness to Ullapool road, 5 miles/8km north of Garve.

Ben Wyvis (3432ft/1046m) is a huge whale-back of a mountain occupying an isolated position above Dingwall and the Moray Firth. It is Inverness's mountain, with easy access from city.

*An Cabar,
Ben Wyvis*

To the west it provides smooth rounded slopes, but to the east it is scalloped into two great corries. It is said that the Earls of Cromarty rented the land from the crown on condition that they could gather a snowball from these corries at any time of year.

The top of the hill is covered in an unusually dense carpet of upland mosses and small mountain plants, and for this reason it has been made a **National Nature Reserve**. It is also home to interesting birds like dotterel and snow bunting.

1 Leave the car park walking north on the new well-made path parallel to the road. Cross a burn on a stout bridge and shortly after this, turn right through a low kissing gate in a deer fence to walk a delightful path high on the bank of the burn. Forest trees lie well back to the sides and the path runs through open heather and scattered birch, with views through to waterfalls below and up to the sharp end ridge (An Cabar) of Ben Wyvis. You may well see siskins up here, and sometimes crossbills.

2 Cross a forest track, where there is a picnic table, and carry on up, through a gate and then another at the end of the young plantation. You are now in the Ben Wyvis National Nature Reserve and an information board tells you about its rare plants and animals. Walk on beside the sparkling burn for a short distance and then wind away to the left with the path, still splendidly surfaced. Ignore a much less attractive wet-looking scar of a path which goes directly up the hillside (the old route). The new path zigzags at an easy gradient up onto a spur, then up it and finally contours to join the old path at the head of the eroded section. The next part of the climb is rocky, with some wet areas and care must be taken to pick a good route among braided paths, but it is

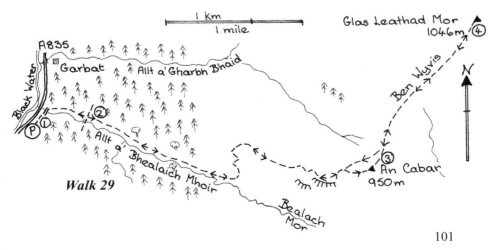

still quite easy. Above a small rise the paths converge, trending over to the right and zigzagging steadily upwards above the Bealach Mor, which separates An Cabar from Little Wyvis. This is a Corbett at 2508ft/764m; soon you can see onto the top of it. A last scramble up a gully takes you onto a rocky eminence, from where it is a gentle stroll up to the top of An Cabar (3115ft/950m).

3 Carry on towards the summit of Ben Wyvis. The walking is easy and delightful, a high level mossy promenade from which you have stunning views over the whole of the north of Scotland. To the north lies a wilderness area; to the south the Moray Firth and Inverness. Dotterel frequent this long whaleback, and ptarmigan can be flushed from its few stony areas; you might even see a golden eagle, mobbed by a peregrine. Cross two small rises and then walk up the final slope to the summit, Glas Leathad Mor, (3429ft/1046m) where the trig point is surrounded by a sheltering wall and there is a fine view down into the eastern corries.

Dotterel

4 When you wish to go down the best way is to retrace your steps. If you do not wish to re-ascend An Cabar there is an obvious small path contouring along the side, which rejoins the upward path on the ridge. Take care as you come to the end of the rocky braided section to find the top of the new path; it is easy to miss, and this would commit you to floundering down the old path.

Practicals

Type of walk: A pleasant climb on a good path for much of the way. The walk along the summit plateau is easy and delightful. It is, however, a Munro and all usual precautions (good boots, waterproofs, map and compass) should be taken. In snow the east edge above the corries develops a cornice, which should be avoided.

Complete distance: 10 miles/16km

Time: 5–6 hours

Maps: OS Explorer 437/Landranger 20

Silverbridge and Black Water

Park at the signed large car park at the south end of the new bridge (Silverbridge), grid ref 402640. It has picnic tables overlooking the river, and toilets. To access this take the A835 (Ullapool road) west from Conon Bridge through Garve and on for 2½ miles/4km.

The **Black Water** is a wild Highland river. On this walk is seen its many rapids, falls and cascades as it tumbles through a lovely gorge between two ancient bridges. In contrast, beyond the second bridge, lie the lush flat pastures of Strath Garve nestling below the steep wooded hillsides of the neighbouring hills and mountains.

Little Garve Bridge

The lower bridge at Little Garve was built around 1762 as part of a military road running from Contin to Poolewe, and is believed to have been constructed by Major Caulfeild, successor to General Wade.

1 From the car park, follow the sign for 'Forest Walks' and bear left to cross the modern road bridge, the Silverbridge. Pause half way to see, upstream, the magnificent cascades as the Black Water rages through confining rocks. At the end of the bridge, descend steps to look at the wonderful lower old bridge and the huge boulder used as a cutwater for it. Go under the new road bridge and climb into a delightful birch wood, with a brilliant green understorey of bilberry, the Black Water now far below.

2 Continue up the hillside on a long flight of easy steps and bear right to go on along a wide forest track below pines. Just beyond a dip, turn right as directed by a green arrow and a post with green and blue encircling bands, to walk a path, covered with pine needles. This descends steadily, then down steps to wind right through more pines where you might spot crossbills high in the trees. Before the path winds right, sit on a seat to look down on a spectacular low waterfall foaming over a constricting rocky outcrop of schist in the riverbed.

3 When you can drag yourself away from this dramatic view, carry on along the good path past more cascades on the burn. Then the path drops down to the riverside and the water flows slowly, having lost some of its tempestuousness. Soon the path begins to rise a little, with heather taking over from bilberry. Below the Black Water finds it way by many routes through huge tilted slabs of schist before suddenly raging on through more rocky projections. Beyond, the second old bridge, with its two arches, comes into view at Little Garve. Continue on the path to take a stile onto a narrow road. Turn right, pausing half

way to look down on the lovely river, wider and calmer now. Then go on over the bridge.

4 Turn right, upstream, along a footpath that leads you beside the river and below some magnificent pines, from where there is a fine retrospective view of the bridge. Go up and down several steps and carry on past all the lovely rapids and cascades seen from the other bank. Look for both grey and pied wagtails, dippers and common sandpipers. At a Y-junction in the path, and if the river isn't too high, take the right branch to follow a little path through great outcrops of schist. Enjoy this idyllic stretch close to the waterfall seen from the seat high on the opposite bank. Follow the continuing good path, soon to pass under the road bridge, then take steps up to the start of the Caulfeild Bridge and go on to where you have parked.

Common sandpiper

Scots Pine

Practicals

Type of walk: A short, glorious walk, on good paths and tracks, along both sides of the splendid Black Water.

Complete distance: 2½ miles/4km

Time: 1–2 hours

Maps: OS Explorer 437/Landranger 20

31

Rogie Falls and View Rock

Park in the forestry car park for Rogie Falls, grid ref 442586. To access these take the A835 for 2 miles/3.4km past Contin in the direction of Garve.

In spate the **Rogie Falls** on the Black Water are most impressive. In low water conditions the river comes down in two falls and then makes a 26ft/8m leap. The Black Water itself has not been affected by the Conon hydro-electric scheme but its headwaters are diverted into it. The falls are crossed by a dramatic suspension bridge from where the best view of the rushing water is obtained.

Rogie Falls

The **salmon ladder** was constructed after the Glascarnoch
Dam was built higher up the river,
because this restricted the flow
of water and at times there was
not enough water in the falls for
the fish to get up. It consists of a
series of pools and small falls
cut into the rock at the side of
the main fall.

Salmon

1   Walk out of the car park by the corner opposite the entry, and descend
    a pleasant path through a narrow valley. At a Y-junction go left. Climb
    a steep bank using a wide zigzag to avoid increasing erosion. The path
    meanders through open larch and birch woodland full of enormous
    boulders, with mosses, ferns and lichens. You may see a great spotted
    woodpecker or at the right time of year hear it drumming. Soon you can
    hear the river, the Black Water, and the path winds down to its bank. Turn
    right and wander along beside the surging water with the roar of the wa-
    terfall growing steadily louder. There is a fine view of the splendid falls
    from the
    bank
    above,
    then a
    walled
    viewpoint,
    and then
    down steps to
    cross a suspen-
    sion bridge over
    the gorge, which
    gives the best view of
    all. Climb steps at the far
    side, above the fish ladder
    where you may see salmon
    jumping, and then follow
    the slanting path left up the
    hill.

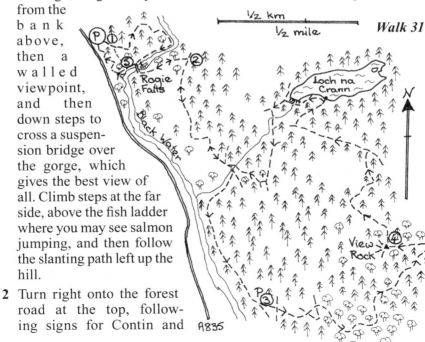

Walk 31

2   Turn right onto the forest
    road at the top, follow-
    ing signs for Contin and

107

Strathpeffer. This is a pleasant, fairly level track with open views out over the valley of the River Conon. A track joins from the left at a wide turning place where there is a seat; just beyond this cross a burn and take a small path on the right, signed for Riverside Walk. Go down beside the burn that descends in a series of falls and waterslides. When you can see the Black Water below, the path winds left along a level river terrace and joins a wider path which leads into another forest car park.

Whooper swans

3 Walk to the information board at the far side of the car park and bear left across a picnic area following a sign for Forest Walks. Wind right at the far side and climb the hill, crossing a forest track and continuing at the far side. Cross the track (which zigzags) twice more and walk on into lovely open birch woodland. Bear left into conifers and climb again; all the way up there are frequent open areas, usually with birch but sometimes with beech or oak. Go round a sharp left bend and climb steeply through dense conifers to a bench at the top in open birch woodland. A short distance further on is View Rock, a huge projecting outcrop of schist. From here there is a fine view of the hills round Strathconon and Loch Achilty, and of Ben Wyvis behind you, but soon the trees are going to need trimming or the view will be lost.

4 Carry on downhill, past an open area where there is another seat, and round a hillside through mature pines. Continue to a path junction and turn left for Contin and Garve. At the next junction there are no signs but take the right branch, crossing a boggy area on duckboards and, beyond a little hill, you reach the shore of Loch na Crann, where there is a small boathouse. This is a lovely quiet loch surrounded by

trees, with tufted duck and whooper swans in winter. Turn left and wind along its shore to the small earth dam at the end. Cross the bridge over the outflow burn and join a forest road where you turn left. About 55yds/50m downhill go left again on a path which re-crosses the burn and winds on down beside it. Ignore a path on your left, but shortly after crossing a tiny burn look for a narrow path on the right and go down this through broom and gorse. Turn right on a wider track which brings you to a ford with stepping stones. Cross, join the forest track beyond and turn right to retrace your steps to Rogie Falls which are just as good the second time of viewing.

5   After crossing the suspension bridge turn left up steps and follow the fenced riverbank downstream. Then climb steeply up steps to a fine viewpoint, Raven's Crag. From here the path carries on climbing until eventually it crosses the top of a knoll and runs back down to the car park.

Tufted ducks

Practicals

Type of walk: A fine forest walk mostly on paths with some tracks.

Complete distance: 4 miles/6.5km
Time: 2–3 hours
Maps: OS Explorer 437/Landranger 26

32

Strathpeffer and Knockfarrel

Park in the large car park in the centre of Strathpeffer, grid ref 483582. Access is along the A834 from Dingwall to Contin.

Strathpeffer was a popular Victorian Spa due to the discovery of mineral springs in the 18th century. People flocked to the town to 'take the waters' to cure their various ailments. With the arrival of the railway at Dingwall, in 1862, more visitors arrived. The town is situated in a wooded valley in Ross-shire. Its name comes from the valley or Strath of the river Peffery. Nowadays it is a charming base when walking in, or touring, the Highlands.

Legend says that if the **Eagle Stone**, carved with Pictish insignia, should fall three times, then ships would be able to anchor on the spot where it last stood. It has already fallen twice and just in case the legend might become reality Strathpeffer has had the stone cemented down. The way to the Eagle Stone is signposted.

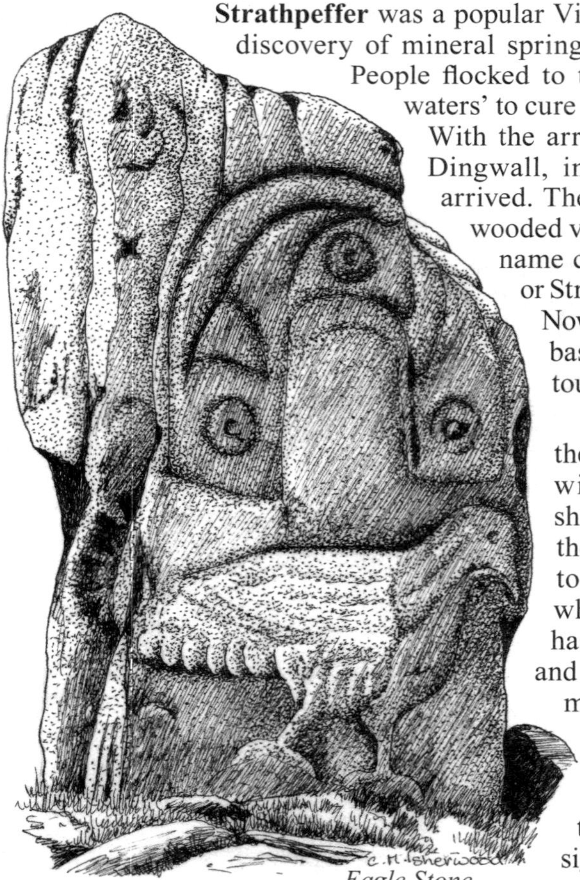

Eagle Stone

110

1 Walk out to the main road and turn right along the pavement past the Spa Pavilion and the Pump house. Admire these fine examples of Victorian Architecture. Carry on up the hill with gardens on your left and houses to your right. At a large house, formerly the Youth Hostel, turn left following footpath signs then immediately turn right on a small path running along the edge of a wood. Keep on along this path until you reach the edge of Jamestown. There is a fine ruined church in a garden ahead but there is no access to it and no access from the path into Jamestown. Wind left following the waymarks and begin the long climb up the edge of the forest with fields across the wall to your right. Look out for red kites quartering the ground in the fields searching for food, and admire their elegant manoeuvring.

2 Cross a stile near the top of the wood to walk up the edge of clear-fell. At the top of this there is a waymark and two paths. The left one is very steep and follows the fence up through young conifers and gorse; the right one contours easily at first and then climbs gently – but at the time of writing is very overgrown with gorse, so much so that a pair of secateurs would be a useful thing to carry with you. This bad bit does not go on for very long; soon you reach a wider more open path at a signpost. Turn left and continue climbing gently, then take a left turn signed to Cnoc Mor and wind on up to the trig point where you join the other path. There is a splendid view through the trees to the hills around Strathconon.

3 Return to the signpost and turn left. The path contours the hill at first and then gradually descends, and whilst a little overgrown in places is easy to follow. There is a fine outlook to the east over Loch Ussie to the Cromarty Firth. Wind down into coniferous forest to a gate where there is a T-junction. Turn left and

after 22yds/20m further on at a signpost go right through a small gate and up a wide clear path leading to open heathery hillside. This is an airy promenade high above Strathpeffer and Strathconon with stunning views in all directions. A memorial on the left commemorates the money raised by the children of Strathpeffer for the earthquake victims in Armenia. Carry on the wonderful high walkway as more of the ridge comes into view ahead. At last you can see the final slope up to Knockfarrel and the distinct shape of the Iron Age Fort. At a fork in the path, go left downhill to a car park. Cross and climb up the far side to the fort. It is vitrified and pieces of the rock showing the characteristic glassy clinker can be seen all round the edges.

4 Explore this fine fort in its splendid situation then return to the car park and take the signed path down the north west side of the hill. At a Y-junction take the right branch, a pleasant path leading down through bracken to another signpost below a Scots pine. Here turn right and go downhill over a stile and on down a long outrake between fences. At the next signpost turn left over a bridge and stile and walk gently uphill along a bank with a ditch to your left until you come to a path slanting away to your right down the field. At the time of writing the waymark is lying in the ditch. Walk down the slanting way heading for the lower end of a belt of trees. Go over a stile beside a gate at the bottom and turn left to walk the old railway line. Pass through a farm gate and traverse the next bit with care; if the farmer has had cows in here it can be quite muddy. Soon you reach a small gate beside a larger one and the track beyond is much easier. Then the station buildings appear through the trees. Walk up onto the platform and admire the lovely Victorian buildings with a very fine glass canopy. There is a café here. Then walk out of the station to the road, cross and turn right. Twenty metres further on there is a gap in the beech hedge and a path leads uphill. Follow this and soon turn right up a smaller path, which will bring you to the Eagle Stone.

Red Kite

5 Return down to

the main path and turn right uphill. Bear left on a road at the top and wind left to come out onto the main road opposite the entrance to the Ben Wyvis Hotel. Turn right and walk back up the main street to your car.

Heather

C.M. Isherwood

Practicals

Type of walk: Very fine, mostly on good clear paths although there is a short struggle through the gorse at present to reach the top of Cnoc Mor. It is worth it for the excellent views.

Complete distance: 6 miles/9.5km

Time: 3–4 hours

Maps: OS Explorer 437/Landranger 26

33

Ord Hill and Kilmuir

Park 306yds/300m up the forest track in a car park on the left, grid ref 656488. Access this by the A9 from Inverness. Take the first minor road on the left, signed to North Kessock and Charlestown, after crossing the Kessock Bridge. Then turn immediately right for Drumsmittal and drive under the A9. Turn left. (From the north there is no problem, just turn left for Drumsmittal.) After 500yards/462m turn right opposite a school, then left at a right-angled bend and right onto the forest track.

Kessock Bridge is a high-level suspension bridge that allows a navigable waterway below. It crosses the Beauly Firth, an inlet of the Moray Firth, and carries the dual carriageway, the A9, connecting the village of North Kessock with Inverness. Construction began in 1976 and was completed in 1982. Four towers dominate the skyline. The bridge replaced a ferry, which had operated for centuries.

Kilmuir and Ord Hill

Red kite re-introduction scheme; the Black Isle was one of the early areas to be used and now about 40 pairs breed around here, although they are still persecuted to some extent and have not spread as far as was hoped.

1 Walk on up the hill following red waymarkers. At a track junction take a small path ahead through a fence gap and up steps. Carry on up the distinct waymarked path and go left at another waymark and on up to the top of the ridge. Immediately before a bench take a path on the left, also red waymarked, which runs along the ridge through open pine forest. Then climb, by steps, the hill ahead, to reach a mound of boulders, which forms the outer wall of a vitrified fort. Go on along the

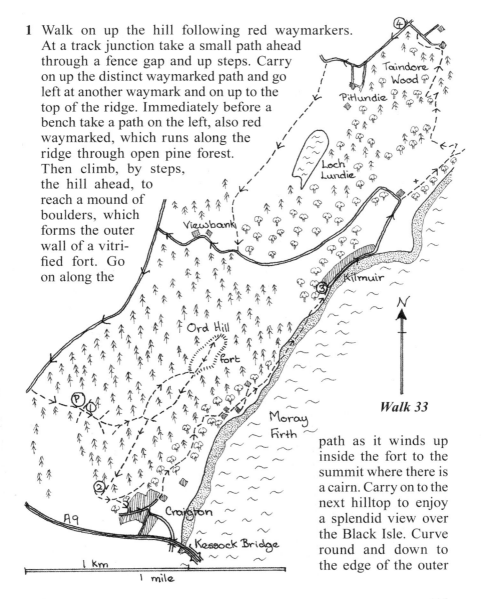

Walk 33

path as it winds up inside the fort to the summit where there is a cairn. Carry on to the next hilltop to enjoy a splendid view over the Black Isle. Curve round and down to the edge of the outer rampart and bear right to follow it. You can climb up to the first summit again or contour round below the top to rejoin your upward path near the heap of stones. Return down the steps and take the left branch still red waymarked; turn left again at a cross of tracks. This path runs downhill through a shallow valley until it reaches a fork where a blue waymarked path goes left to a viewpoint from where there is a fine view of Inverness and the Kessock Bridge. Return to your downward path and carry on to descend steps to a wide forest track.

2 Turn left. About 100yds/91m further on, directly above the Kessock Bridge, look for a small path on the right going steeply down the bank to an old gate beside a yellow-topped fence post, and a path going downhill beyond. This emerges among houses in the village of Craigton. Turn right at a road, then left at a junction and follow this road down between the cottages to a hairpin bend to the right. There is a wide bay with No Parking signs. A road labelled Private runs straight on ahead and to its left is a small path with a red kite waymark. Go along here with the fence to your right. It is a most beautiful path running through open beech wood with extensive views out over the Moray Firth. Eventually it begins to slope downhill. Ignore a path going uphill to the left and carry on down, winding round the hillside, to a fence. Walk along above the fence and then between a house and its outbuildings, round the end and onto a metalled drive. Go on down to a junction where the metalled road turns right and is marked Private. Continue ahead down a track towards the shore, past a ruined boathouse and then on along a small path. This runs along the top of the shore but at times goes down onto the pebbles; it would be difficult at high tides and impassable at high springs. After a short distance, at a signpost, steps join it from the left. Go on along the shore or behind it, sometimes in gullies behind boulders, until you reach the village of Kilmuir, picturesquely situated around a bay. Go under a bridge to a garden deck and onto the end of the road.

3 Walk along the road in front of the cottages then uphill to a bend with houses and a farm steading. A signpost here directs you past a cemetery and the ivy-covered ruins of St. Mary's Church, then down the bank through deciduous trees. At a field gate ignore a small gate on the right with a kite waymark and instead go through into the field. Shut the gate carefully and look for several red kites soaring overhead. Look closely at the sea here in winter where you may see flocks of long-tailed ducks. There is gorse on the left in the field so walk along the track until it stops and then turn left and climb up parallel to the fence. Then walk along the top of the field, going round gorse thickets,

and through a gate in the far corner to climb a ladder stile over the fence to your left. Drop down a few steps to your left onto an old path running up through the wood to a hairpin bend. Wind right and ascend through lovely deciduous woodland to join a path outside the garden fence of Taindore House. Turn left and walk up the path until your way is blocked by an old gate. Go left here up a small path into the wood and follow it through heather and bilberry to join a wider path. Walk right, down to the entrance track to Taindore just outside its gate. Turn left, continue along the track to a metalled road and turn left again.

Long-tailed ducks

4 Walk down the road through woodland with a reed-bed to the right. Bend right, then left and at a signpost take the fenced path on the left which climbs the hill. Go through a small gate and along the top of the field, with Loch Lundie below to your left and Ord Hill ahead. Beyond another gate the track descends and becomes grassy. Step over a stile below a large pine and carry on down a narrow fenced path. At the bottom go over another stile and out onto a road. Turn right and walk uphill to a junction. Turn left here and walk back along the narrow road to the entrance to the forestry car park. Go left again and uphill to your car.

Practicals

Type of walk: Pleasantly varied with pine and deciduous forest, seashore, open fields and a small loch. There are fine wide views out over the Moray Firth. The paths are mostly clear but there are some fields to cross; please close gates and keep dogs on leads. At high tides the shore path to Kilmuir will not be passable.

Complete distance: 7 miles/11.4km

Time: 3–4 hours

Maps: OS Explorer432/Landranger 26

34

Rosemarkie and Chanonry Point

Park in a parking area on the right, at the north end of the charming small village of Rosemarkie, grid ref 737576. To reach this, leave the A9 at Tore to take the A832 through Fortrose, very soon to reach the village.

Chanonry Point lies at the end of Chanonry Ness, a spit of land extending into the Moray Firth between Fortrose and Rosemarkie on the Black Isle. It 'faces' Fort George across the Firth and is one of the best places to watch bottle-nosed dolphins for which the Moray Firth is noted.

Fort George, completed by 1769, stands on a promontory jutting into the Moray Firth, opposite Chanonry Point. Around the 1600 infantry garrison a mile of boundary walls were constructed. It was built in readiness for any trouble that might arise from the Scots, but trouble never came. It is still functioning as a garrison today and you might wish, later, to visit the Regimental Museum of the Queen's Own Highlanders (Seaforths and Camerons).

Fortrose Cathedral

Fairy Glen is an RSPB reserve and is noted for its

plants as well as its woodland birds. Moschatel, sanicle, woodruff and ramsons all grow well here but are uncommon in the surrounding area.

1   Leave the parking area by a gap at the north end, cross the road and take the signposted footpath opposite, signed "Swallow Den Walk to Fortrose, 1¼ miles". The little path takes you up through deciduous woodland with, at first, several small sections being stepped and followed by a longer flight of steps. Continue on a boardwalk, just after a particularly muddy area. Gorse, larch and cherry slope down to the dell on your right. The path heads on up through gorse and larch through a glorious strip of woodland, with pasture to the left and an immensely deep hollow to the right, the latter densely clad in deciduous trees. Then follows a short steep part of the path, where walking poles are a help. Once up, the delightful way becomes more level and through the gaps in the gorse, to the left, you have an extensive view over Fortrose and Chanonry Point, and across the narrows to Fort George on the opposite side of the Moray Firth. Follow the path as it winds steadily left, through elms and cherry, with an understorey of salmonberry and wood rush, to join a narrow road.

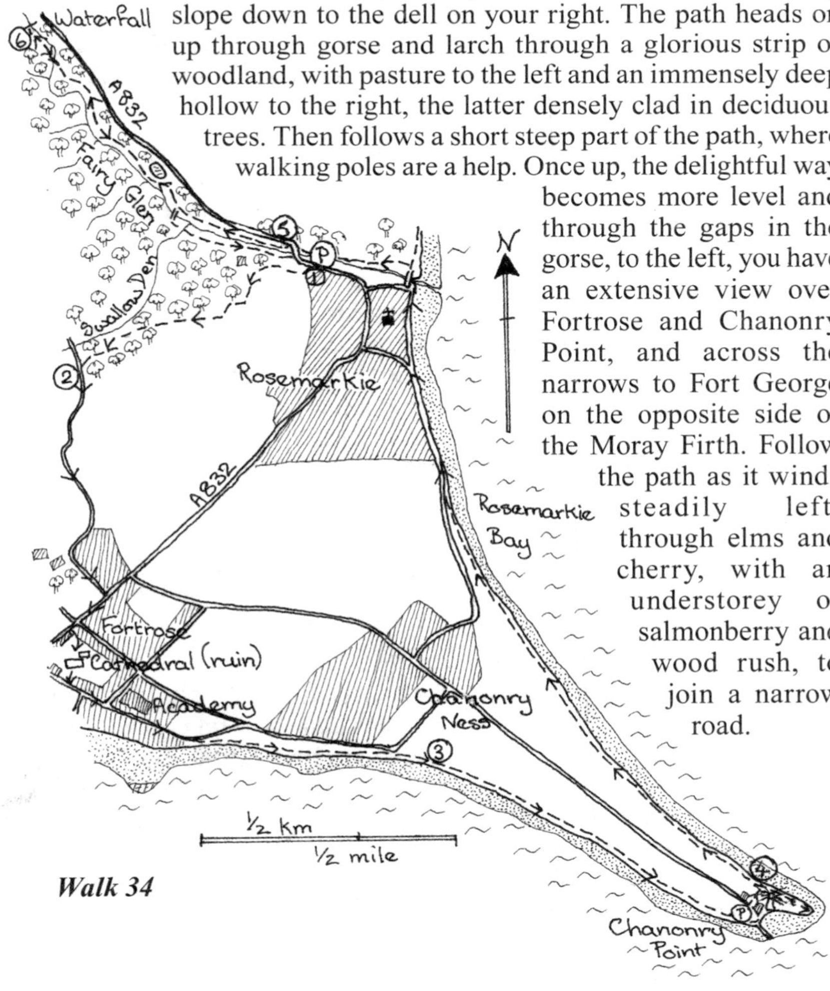

Walk 34

119

2 Descend left as it drops very steeply towards Fortrose. In spring the way is edged with a colourful array of flowers and linnets serenade you as you go. At the main road of the charming town, turn right to pass a church and then cross the road and follow a sign directing you left, and then right, to the Cathedral, a pleasing ruin you might wish to visit. Once in its grounds, wind right and eventually leave by the gate below the clock tower. Continue on left along a quiet road. Go past the Episcopalian church and then Fortrose Academy. Carry on down the road with gorse hedging to your right and the Firth beyond. Soon you reach a grassy area with picnic tables, where you might like a pause and enjoy the sea views. Then join a hedged path that goes on above the shore from where there are more pleasing views. Pass through a camping and caravanning site, keeping along the grassy way just above the shore.

3 Soon, if the tide is high, you will have to move away from the beach. Continue on beside a small parking area. Wind round, left, behind the lighthouse (now a private house) turn right alongside it to reach the spit, where there are more picnic tables and an area much used by dolphin spotters.

4 After a break here, walk the sandy shore with patches of shingle, on along the lovely curving bay, keeping an eye open for dolphins, and enjoying the wild flowers and the bird life. In winter you may see long-tailed duck and both great and Arctic skuas in autumn. When the shore becomes all shingle and quite uncomfortable to walk, move left up to a sandy path, with a golf course beyond the gorse. Carry on towards the houses of Rosemarkie, and then past them, to reach the end of the road. After crossing over the Fairy Glen Burn you may wish to go on to the beach café, which has toilets. Otherwise turn left, away from the sea, and walk beside the burn. Go under a very low bridge, enjoy the spectacular sandstone cliffs rearing up to your right, and walk on beside the burn to pass under the road bridge.

5 Follow the well kept path into the tree-clad steep-sided glen. Ignore a bridge over the burn, climb a few steps and carry on past a mill-pond, where once flax was steeped, and where you might spot herons and mallards. Continue beside a leat to come beside the burn once more. Further on the burn makes a large curve and the path carries straight ahead through the glorious woodland. It then narrows and comes to a bridge, which you cross. Climb steps, wind along the path to reach the splendid Fairy Glen Falls where two long tresses of water descend into a plunge pool then drop down in dramatic cascades before dancing down the glen.

6 Return along the path, past the mill pond and on to the bridge you ignored nearer the start of the walk. This time you do cross to walk back along the other side of the pretty burn. After walking a raised walkway, join a metalled access track and then 100yds/90m before the road, descend four steps on the left to walk beside the burn again. Pass under the road bridge and rejoin your vehicle.

Moschatel

Practicals

Type of walk: Delightful – a little bit of everything. Mainly level except for the steepish climb at the start. Just take your time.

Complete distance: 6½ miles/10.5km

Time: 4 hours

Maps: OS Explorer 432/Landranger 27

35

South Sutor and MacFarquhar's Bed from Cromarty

Park in the large parking area close to the shore, at the foot of High Street in Cromarty village, grid ref 789676. To access the village leave the A9 as it crosses the Black Isle and take the A832 for Fortrose and Cromarty.

Cromarty is a charming ancient town that lies at the tip of the Black Isle. The present town dates mainly from the 18th century and is a delightful blend of sturdy mansions and fishermen's cottages. It has had many economic setbacks in its past, such as the decline of the herring fishery in the early 18th century, then the failure to compete with mechanized factories in the south. Later, when the railway came north Dingwall and Invergordon were favoured to the disadvantage of Cromarty. It was an important naval base in both World Wars but then followed another decline. Cromarty's economy revived in the 1970s with the development of the oil related industries and the building of the Kessock Bridge.

Early on the walk you pass into a SSI made famous by **Hugh Miller,** writer, stonemason and geologist. As a boy and then as a

Hugh Millers's Cottage

stonemason he had always been curious about the nature of the landscape. In the autumn of 1830 he undertook a thorough survey of the landform of the Cromarty Firth. He discovered the famous fossil fish beds and he then went on to make an important contribution to the understanding of Old Red Sandstone.

MacFarquhar was a pirate and a smuggler in the Cromarty area. His 'Bed' from which he used to spy out his victims is a huge crag of rock with an arch hollowed out by the sea.

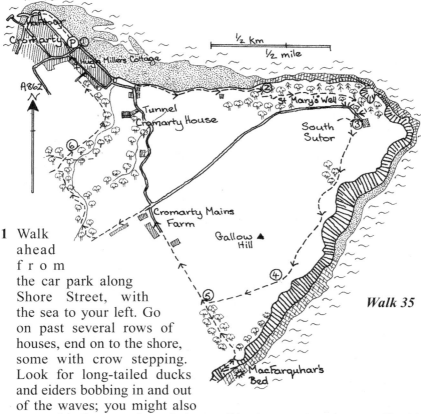

Walk 35

1 Walk ahead from the car park along Shore Street, with the sea to your left. Go on past several rows of houses, end on to the shore, some with crow stepping. Look for long-tailed ducks and eiders bobbing in and out of the waves; you might also see seals. Then turn inland along Miller Street, past a house still with the remnants of a hoist of an old mill. At the corner, where the road turns inland again, take a ginnel, left, towards the shore and a signpost. Follow the arm for 'Sutors of Cromarty' to walk a lovely path beside the Firth, with a field to the right. At low tide you can see the shale

beds where Hugh Miller found his fossil fish. At the next signpost go straight ahead.

2 Then the path winds into deciduous woodland, through carpets of wood rush and you begin your climb of the 'hundred steps'. These are well-maintained wooden steps with long ramps between and the occasional bridge, with the land sloping very steeply up to your right and also steeply down to the shore. Through the trees you have glimpses of the sea and North Sutor. There are several seats on which to pause as you make the long, splendid climb. Go past St Mary's Well. After about the first seventy steps the path runs along a terrace through mixed woodland. There are several concrete remains left from wartime defences and in one place a fenced path runs above a vertical concrete buttress. The last few steps lead to a sturdy wooden signpost and a sandy car park, where you turn left.

3 Go through a kissing gate as directed by the signpost (to MacFarquhar's Bed), with a fine view of the Moray Firth ahead. A few steps from the gate, and just beyond a clump of gorse, join a rough path over a pasture. This is part of the Cromarty Trail, which has not yet been developed. It is quite hard walking because cattle have poached the ground and a tractor has churned up the path, but skylarks fill the air with songs and all seems well with the world. Continue to a gate, which you will have to climb if you cannot untie it, and walk on ahead over more rough pasture also used earlier by cows. If the gorse is in bloom, the breeze off the sea picks up its perfume and carries it towards you.

4 Pass through two large iron gates and walk ahead across a pasture on a delightful path. Follow it as it bears half right to the top right corner of a wood. Go through the gate and turn left to descend through the wide ribbon of open woodland, edged with ancient beeches. This brings you to a grassy area just before the fenced cliff. Step over the fence in the right corner – the stile has disappeared – and pause on the bench seat to enjoy this lovely stretch of high cliffs. From here you might be able to spot Fort George and Chanonry Point, both overlooking the Moray Firth. If you wish to reach MacFarquhar's Bed and if you have a good head for heights, follow the little path as it winds right and then sharply left and descends steeply, zigzagging down the steep cliff face. Much of the path has gorse on both sides, but in two places you can look dizzily down a long way. After exploring the shore and stacks, only possible if the tide is right, return up the cliff and through the wood to reach the gate at the ridge. Pause here to see both the Cromarty Firth and the Moray Firth, having walked round the tip of the Black Isle.

5 Ignore the gate used earlier and pass through one ahead; go along a wide sandy path at the edge of a field, past a cowshed, then through a small gate onto a road with houses to your left. Walk on down to reach Cromarty Mains Farm beyond which you turn left. Continue on the farm track, past bungalows, until you reach woodland on the right. Here

Eiders

take a little path into the trees. Follow this lovely way and keep a look out for roe deer. On reaching a wide track, turn right with woodland on both sides and then a field to the left. At a cross of tracks, ignore a track left and right and also the one straight ahead which goes into the field; go ahead to the right of this one to walk an easy-to-miss footpath just inside more woodland, with a fence to your left and a field beyond it.

6 Carry on through the trees with a little burn to your right, which soon flows on out of sight in its deep gorge. Go on along the path as it winds left and passes through a glade surrounded by huge beeches. Pass through a small gate with ahead a view of the now roofless Gaelic Chapel and Hugh Miller monument, which was erected in 1859. Descend to a road, and turn right to walk The Paye. Bear left into Church Street to pass the thatched Hugh Miller's house (1711) and then the fine Courthouse (1773). Wind right at the High Street to return to the car park.

Practicals

Type of walk: Very pleasing. The South Sutor is a joy to climb and the views of the two Firths a delight. Take care if you visit MacFarquhar's Bed.

Complete distance: 5 miles/8km
Time: 3 hours
Maps: OS Explorer 432/Landranger 21

36

The Black Rock Gorge of Novar

Park in the well signposted car park off the main street of the village of Evanton, grid ref 608661. This is accessed from the A9, north of the Cromarty bridge, along the B817.

The **Black Rock Gorge** of Novar is 1 mile/1.5km long, 100ft/30m deep and barely 12ft/4m wide. It was formed during the last ice age when glacial meltwater from Ben Wyvis flowed down the valley of Glen Glass, heavily laden with erosive sand and gravel cutting rapidly through a resistant band of Old Red Sandstone conglomerate. The gorge is on the 21,000 acre **Novar Estate** owned by the Munro-Fergusson Family. The top of the ravine is covered with moss, ferns and saplings and over-shadowed by lichen-covered conifers of Evanton Wood. Here the river is known as the Allt Graad. Higher up it is named the River Glass.

In 2004 Warner Brothers were in Evanton, filming around the Black Rock Gorge for possible use as the back drop for **'Harry Potter and the Goblet of Fire'**, where Harry is chased by the dragon.

Black Rock Gorge

Walk 36

1 Cross the road from the car park and walk right (north). Go past the Novar Arms, the church and the camping and caravan park, to cross the bridge over the river. Turn left up a quiet lane, signed to Glen Glass and Assynt and continue up-hill to a Y-junction. Here take the left branch and carry on to pass a house, on the right, named Balavoulin.

Wild garlic

2 After a mile from the bridge and beyond Balavoulin, take a wide track, descending left, through fine mixed woodland. Ignore a track on the left. Emerge from the trees and continue ahead on a narrower path, with splendid Assynt House, right, above a sheep grazed pasture. Follow the path as it suddenly winds left into fenced woodland to take a fenced footbridge over the Black Rock gorge. Only those walkers with a head for heights will be able to pause long on the bridge and look down into the narrow depths below, considered one of Scotland's geological wonders.

3 Once across turn left and walk the fenced way to reach a second bridge, which you do not cross – though you might wish to stand on it for another glimpse of the incredible depths through which the river hurries or, go to the far end for a best view upstream and to see the depth of the ravine.

4 Go on up a wide track through the forest. At the top of the slope, at a T-junction, turn left to walk a delightful wide way that descends, almost imperceptibly, through the lovely Evanton Wood. Look for siskins in the trees. Where the track winds gently right you can see, beyond the river far below, a splendid waterfall, but keep well back from the edge of the gorge.

5 Carry on down the way to a cross of tracks, where you wind left, with fields to the left and woodland to the right. From here you have a good view of the Cromarty Firth. At the road, turn left and walk down the sloping way to the main road through the village, where you turn right for the signed car park.

Coal tit

Practicals

Type of walk: Some quiet road walking and then a short walk through pleasing woodland to an incredibly deep gorge. Here small children/youngsters should be under tight control. The return brings you back to Evanton on forest tracks through more fine woodland.

Complete distance: 2½ miles/4km
Time: 2 hours
Maps: OS Explorer432/Landranger 21

37

Fyrish Hill

Park in the small car park, grid ref 627715. To access this going north, leave the A9 north-east of Evanton and turn left onto the B9176, signed to Alness and Bonar Bridge. After two miles take the unclassified road, on the left, signed Boath. A mile along this road you reach the car park on your left.

Fyrish Monument was built by the local laird, Sir Hector Munro of Novar. He was Commander of the successful British Forces in India. He returned to his estate just at the time of the Highland clearances when many people were starving. At that time famine relief was provided only for work. He set the local people to build the monument on the Fyrish Hill. It is a replica of **the gates of Negapataum**, where the laird had his last victory. All the stones were carried to the summit. After the locals had finished he arranged for all the great stones to be rolled down the hill again. These were then taken up once more by the local people and Sir Hector was able to pay the workers twice. The irony of it all was that he organized the area to be turned into a great sheep run.

Monument, Fyrish Hill

1 Leave by the large wooden kissing gate into the extensive pine woodland. This is known as the Jubilee path. It is lined with heather, juniper, bilberry, wood rush and bog myrtle and is a delight to walk. The track climbs gently through the well spread pines allowing light to the undergrowth. Cross a wide track and continue on as directed by the waymark. The route then descends stone steps to a footbridge over a

Walk 37

½ km

½ mile

Cnoc
Fyrish
453m
Monument

very deep narrow ravine, its sides clothed by lush vegetation all the way down to the Contullich Burn. More steps carry on up to the continuing track. Siskins fly overhead and coal tits whisper from the trees.

2 Go on over the next cross of tracks where the pines begin to open out and you have a wonderful view down the Cromarty Firth to the Black Isle. Carry on ahead over another cross of tracks. To the left you can see a pretty lochan. Then as you press on up and up, the pines are less tall and much more scattered, the path swinging left and then winding right. Look for green hairstreak butterflies flitting across the track. The way levels and continues through high moorland, with vast acres of heather to the right and a magnificent view, left, down the lovely valley to the Cromarty Firth, with the Cairngorms in the distance. Head on the stony way to reach the incredible monument, where you will want to pause and enjoy the superb view.

Green hairstreak butterfly

3 Return for a few steps to a direction sign which points to the way you came up. If you wish to take a more challenging descent ignore this sign and take a wide track going off left beside the sign. At first this is a flat easy way, heather-lined, along the continuing ridge from where you have an extensive view of the mountains. Where it begins to wind steeply down and has been washed out by the winter rains, descend the easier path through the heather to the right. Go on down until you reach a Y-junction and take another easier short track down to the next bend that has also been washed out. Now you are reaching a scattering of pines. Descend another steepish area, taking care on the 'ball-bearing' stones to reach a more enclosed area and a pleasing track that is once more a pleasure to walk.

4 At the waymark go ahead until you reach the cross of tracks, walked over on the way up. Here turn left and follow the track to cross the bridge over the narrow ravine. Go over the next cross of track, to descend to the car park where you might well spot a buzzard in the conifers.

Buzzard

Practicals

Type of walk: Most pleasing. Parts of the way can be a little arduous, but take your time. Enjoy the magnificent monument.

Complete distance: 4 miles/6.5km
Time: 3–4 hours
Maps: OS Explorer 438/Landranger 21

38

The Struie and Struie Hill

Park at the top of the B9176 from Alness to Bonar Bridge, about ½ mile/1 km south of the viewpoint at the Cadha Mor, in a large space on the west of the road, grid reference 651851.

From the summit of Struie Hill you can see a long stretch of **Dornock Firth**, the most northerly of the three great firths that penetrate the east side of the Northern Highlands. Small hills overlook the Firth, the most prominent one being Struie Hill topped by a communication mast.

Kyle of Sutherland from the Struie

1   Walk north up the road for about 50yds/45m and just before a road sign look for a rather obscure path on the right, before a clump of willow bushes. There is an awkward step across a deep ditch, but then the path becomes more distinct, winding round the willows and then going straight uphill to the left of a narrow pinewood. Grouse scatter and croak as you climb. As you approach the top the slope steepens, ending

N

Struie Hill
331m.

Cadha Mor
Viewpoint

1 Km

1 mile

P

Struie
373m.

B9176

in a rocky staircase, which emerges onto the summit of the Struie. Walk left along the path up to the cairn. This is the highest point on the ridge and the views are superb, especially to the left looking up the Kyle of Sutherland to the distant Ben More Assynt, almost on the west coast.

Red grouse

2 Continue along the top of the long narrow ridge. The path is distinct to begin with. After a while you descend into a dip and here take the left fork, even though this looks less obvious than the right one. Climb a sharp rise and go past a pool on your right. Continue on to a cairn on the northern edge, and enjoy the splendid view. Carry on gradually descending, mainly keeping towards the left side of the ridge. At times the path disappears but if you look around it is always possible to pick it up again. As it goes down to the lowest col before the final top, Struie Hill, it does become very obscure and is rather mixed up with a watercourse; this is made worse because people have used this slope for scramble biking. However the track up the final slope is very obvious so keep that in view and take one of the many paths towards it. Then climb the rocky track to the summit where there is a telecommunications mast. From here you can see the whole of the Dornoch Firth to Tarbat Ness as well as across to the western mountains – a really fantastic view.

3 Return by your outward path, leaving the track about 20yds/18m before a sharp left bend and picking up the path. It is easier to see

where it goes in this direction. As you walk along the ridge look for hen harriers hunting low over the heather. On reaching the higher summit (Struie) descend the steep slope to return to your car.

Hen harrier

Practicals

Type of walk: Many excellent views. It is all on paths but in some places they are rather obscure and can be wet. The climbs are quite steep.

Complete distance: 5 miles/8km
Time: 3 hours
Maps: OS Explorer 438/Landranger 21

The Aldie Burn

From the Tain bypass, take the road signposted Scotsburn. After two miles, turn right following the Forest Enterprise signs for the forest walks. Aldie Burn car park, grid ref 758793, is reached ⅛ mile/200m along this track.

The **Aldie burn** flows through mixed conifer forest and pleasant open woodland, with many gnarled old pines. The two walks, mainly beside the burn, have been recently upgraded to "Countryside for All" standards, suitable for prams and wheelchairs. The Pond trail takes about 20 minutes to walk and the Burn Trail, 2 miles/3.4m long, about 1hours 20 minutes. There is a picnic area but no toilets.

The handsome **Capercaillie** may be seen on this walk. It was introduced to this country in 1837, though the bird is indigenous but had died out. It is a native of most European pine forests and the ancestors of the

Aldie Burn

C.M.Isherwood

present birds came from Sweden. In the remote past the capercallie made fine meals for our ancestors.The male capercaillie has black upper parts and underparts, the latter speckled with grey. The feathers of the neck are elongated and spread out during display. It has feathered legs and a green gorget. Above the eye is a long vermillion wattle, the heavy bill is yellowish. The female is a smaller reddish brown bird but still very large. In early spring the male fights other males and, if triumphant, performs an extravagant display for the entertainment and benefit of admiring hens, making a characteristic popping, clacking noise that may be the source of its name, which translates as 'horse of the woods'.

Capercaillie (displaying)

1 From the parking area follow the signed track into woodland. Turn right at a forest track and then left at a T-junction. Cross a small stream and wind left along a raised path beneath Douglas fir. Then the woodland opens out and you pass through larch and silver birch. Pass a ring of stones and then more separate stones, part of the 'forest art'. Look

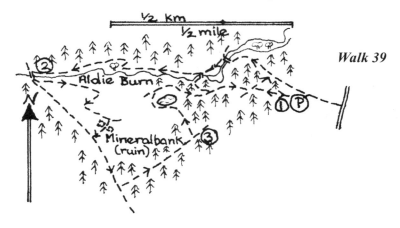

Walk 39

for the pond on the left and perhaps make a pleasant circle of it before returning to the main track, which soon winds right uphill and then continues left above the river in a wide open glen between trees.

2 It then descends and continues to an attractive footbridge, where you will want to pause to look upstream into an open grassy area. After crossing the bridge, follow half-left, a narrower path that winds through more open ground where flowers colour the way. After quarter of a mile the path bears right, and leads past an old ruined farm steading called Mineralbank. Carry on along the path until it joins a forest road. Climb, left, uphill for another quarter of a mile to a T-junction where you turn left along a wide forest road, with trees set back on either side.

3 After another quarter of a mile, turn left again to descend a narrower way through the glorious woodland. Go with it as it curves left round another pond, where you may see mallards in the reeds, and then right to join a good track. Here bear right and follow this track back past the first pond and then along above the Aldie Burn to cross a track and return to the parking area. As you go through the forest look for crossbills feeding on cones in the pine trees and in spring listen for the weird popping call of displaying capercaillies.

Bog Myrtle

Practicals

Type of walk: Short easy walk through a fine forest.

Complete distance: 2 miles/3.4km
Time: 1–2 hours
Maps: OS Explorer 438/Landranger 21

40

Portmahomack and Tarbat Ness

Park in one of the car parks along the front in Portmahomack, grid ref 915844. To access this, leave the A9 about 3 miles/5km south of Tain and follow the B 9165 for Portmahomack. This road makes two right-angled bends but is well signed.

Tarbat Ness lighthouse, designed by Robert Stevenson, was completed in January 1830. At 130ft/40m to the top of the tower and 175ft/53m to the very top it is the third tallest lighthouse in Britain, and the highest on the mainland. North Ronaldsay and Skerryvore are taller.

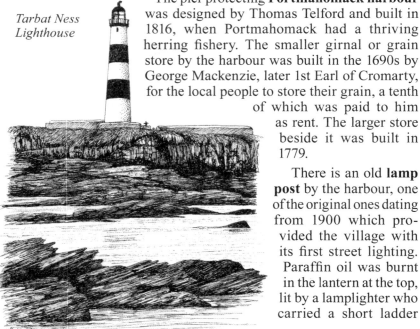

Tarbat Ness Lighthouse

The pier protecting **Portmahomack harbour** was designed by Thomas Telford and built in 1816, when Portmahomack had a thriving herring fishery. The smaller girnal or grain store by the harbour was built in the 1690s by George Mackenzie, later 1st Earl of Cromarty, for the local people to store their grain, a tenth of which was paid to him as rent. The larger store beside it was built in 1779.

There is an old **lamp post** by the harbour, one of the original ones dating from 1900 which provided the village with its first street lighting. Paraffin oil was burnt in the lantern at the top, lit by a lamplighter who carried a short ladder around with him to reach the lights. Funding was provided by entertainments called the Paraffin Concerts. The lights were turned off at the beginning of the 1914-1918 war and not reinstated until 1949.

1 Walk north along the sea front to the harbour designed by Telford, and look at the old grain stores. Continue along the road until it curves right, then carry on along grass in front of bungalows to a wicket gate beside a field gate. There is a distinct path running along above the shore, on the 10ft/3m wave-cut platform, with the low cliffs of the 50 ft/15m wave-cut platform to the right. Head on through a farm gate in a fence, then on behind the shore to a stile over the next fence with a rather boggy area to negotiate beyond. Curlews and oystercatchers frequent the shore, with dunlin, knot and wigeon in winter. Go through the next farm gate and cross the grass inside the fence towards a red-roofed bothy. Just beyond it, follow the track up the hillside but do not keep to the field at the top; drop down a little and walk the delightful grassy platform above the 'cliffy' shore. Cross a stile and go on to a rocky promontory where the platform ends. Go up right to the top of the promontory, then wind right and go through a gap in the dense gorse to reach the field. Turn left and walk on above the gorse until you come to a kissing gate. The top of the lighthouse is visible from here.

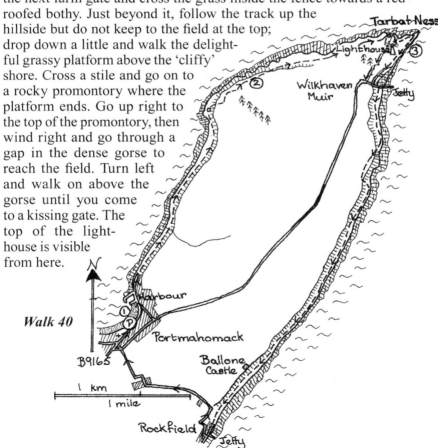

Walk 40

139

2 Press on along the cliff top and through a farm gate after which the path descends gently to shore level again. Look out for hares racing over the grass. Walk along beside a fence with a pond on the right beyond it. You may see greenshank and redshank on the shore and if you are very lucky, an otter. There is a stile over the next fence consisting of a stone on either side and rope binding over the two strands of barbed wire. If you have long legs this is fine. Otherwise go uphill, through the two gates in the fence corner, and down to rejoin the path. The lighthouse is very near now, enclosed by a fine wall which has a gate in it and a 'no entry' sign. If the tide is low turn left and go down the grassy slope to the beach. Cross the pebbles and scramble fairly easily up the sandstone rocks at the far side to round the corner of the lighthouse wall. A small path runs by the wall and then heads off into the heather. At a T-junction turn left. The path runs through maritime heath and then along the top of the shore to the point, where it joins a fine grassy track leading back to the far side of the lighthouse. Here there is an information board about bottle-nosed dolphins. This area is a favourite bird-watching place, with Manx and sooty shearwaters, and Arctic, great and pomarine skuas among the excitements which may come past. If the tide is high it will not be possible to get across to the end of the lighthouse wall. In this case turn right and walk beside the wall to a gate by a small plantation. Go through and on to the next gate where you reach the public road. Turn left. Another left turn will take you past the lighthouse and on to the point; or you can go straight ahead down to the jetty to continue the walk.

Arctic Skua

3 Follow the metalled road from the lighthouse to a car park. Carry on along the road then turn left down to a small jetty. Go through a small gate on the right, along a path through the field beyond and on through marram below low cliffs. Please keep dogs on lead. Soon you can see a rocky promontory ahead; rounding it on the shore is difficult and is not possible at high tide. Pick the easiest of several paths up the grassy slope to the cliff top. Step over a broken gate and follow a small path along an earth bank then across open ground with fields to your right and gorse to the left. Where the fence comes near to the cliff edge again look for a small easy path back down to the shore. From now on the

140

way stays on the low wave-cut platform. Cross a stile over a fence, then round another promontory, the track becomes wider and more obvious. There is a fine towerhouse, Ballone Castle, on the right, in process of restoration at the time of writing. Cross a ladder stile over a stone wall and follow the path through gorse, over a step stile and in front of the first cottage of the little village of Rockfield to join the road. After a few steps, turn right on the road and climb to the top of the cliffs. The minor road winds round and crosses the peninsula. As you come down into Portmahomack it meets the B 9165. Cross and walk down the edge of the grass by a bus stop and then down the road into the village. There is a path behind the shore which you can follow back to your car.

Bottlenose Dolphins

Practicals

Type of walk: Mostly distinct paths although in two places you have to climb up to avoid 'cliffy' areas, and in another the way goes along the shore and would not be passable at high tide, though there is an alternative.

Complete distance: 7 miles/11.4km

Time: 4 hours

Maps: OS Explorer 438/Landranger 21

Walking Scotland Series
from Clan Books

MARY WELSH has already compiled walkers' guides to each of the areas listed: material for guides covering the remaining parts of Scotland is being gathered for publication in future volumes.

Titles published so far:

Books in this series can be ordered through booksellers anywhere.
In the event of difficulty write to
Clan Books, The Cross, DOUNE, FK16 6BE, Scotland.

For more details, visit the Clan Books website at
www.walkingscotlandseries.co.uk